To

_____

From

_____

Message

_____

_____

_____

God's Best Secrets

© 1994 Christian Art Gifts, RSA
        Christian Art Gifts Inc., IL, USA

First edition 1994
Second edition 1999
Third edition 2003

Designed by Christian Art Gifts

Material in this book is adapted from *God's Best Secrets* by Andrew Murray by permission of Kregel Publications.

Unless otherwise indicated, Scripture taken from the *Holy Bible*, King James Version. Copyright © 1962 by The Zondervan Corporation. Used by permission. *Holy Bible*, Revised Version.

ISBN 978-1-86920-134-0

Printed in China

07 08 09 10 11 12 13 14 15 16 – 14 13 12 11 10 9 8 7 6 5

GOD'S BEST SECRETS

One-Minute Devotions

Andrew Murray

JANUARY 1

FROM DAY TO DAY

"The inner man is renewed from day to day."
2 Corinthians 4:16

There is one lesson that all Christians should learn – *the absolute necessity of fellowship with Jesus each day.*

The Lord Jesus will every day from heaven continue His work in me. But on one condition – *the soul must give Him time each day* to impart His love and His grace. Time alone with the Lord Jesus each day is the indispensable condition of growth and power.

The Lord will teach us just how meek and humble He is (Mt. 11:25-20). Bow before Him, tell Him that you long for Him and His love, and He will let His love rest on you.

January 2

Fellowship with God

*"He that loveth Me shall be loved
of my Father. I will love Him."*
John 14:21

God gave Christ His Son *to bring us to Himself*. But this
is only possible when we live in close fellowship with
Jesus Christ.

Our relationship to Christ rests on His deep, tender
love to us. We are not able of ourselves to render Him
this love. But the Holy Spirit will do the work in us. For
this we need to separate ourselves each day from the
world and turn in faith to the Lord Jesus, that He may
shed abroad His love in our hearts, *so that we may be
filled with a great love to Him.*

JANUARY 3

JESUS

*"Thou shalt call His Name Jesus, for
He shall save His people from their sins."*
Matthew 1:21

The living Christ reveals Himself to us, and through the power of His love, the love of sin is expelled. It is through personal fellowship with Him that Jesus saves us from our sins. I must come as an individual, with my heart and all the sin that is in it, to Jesus as an Almighty personal Savior in whom God's holiness dwells.

And as He and I commune together in the expression of mutual love and desire by the work of His Holy Spirit in my heart, His love will expel and conquer all sin.

JANUARY 4

THE INNER CHAMBER

"When thou prayest enter into thine inner chamber."
Matthew 6:6, RV

"Enter into thine inner chamber, and having shut thy door, pray to thy Father which is in secret." That means two things. Shut the world out, withdraw from all worldly thoughts and occupations, and shut yourself in alone with God to pray to Him in secret. Let this be your chief object in prayer, to realize the presence of your heavenly Father.

Prayer in secret will be followed by the secret working of God in my heart.

Prayer in fellowship with Jesus cannot be in vain.

January 5

Faith

"Only believe."
Mark 5:36

We must have *faith in all that God is willing to do for us*. We must have faith each day according to our special needs. God is infinitely great and powerful; Christ has so much grace for each new day that our faith must reach out afresh each day according to the need of the day.

Before you begin to pray, ask yourself, "Do I really believe that *God is here with me, and that the Lord Jesus will help me to pray,* and I may expect to spend a blessed time in communion with my God?"

JANUARY 6

THE WORD OF GOD

"Man shall not live by bread alone, but by every word that proceedeth out of the mouth of God."
Matthew 4:4

A mere knowledge of God's Word will not avail me. It is not enough to think about it, I must feed on God's Word and take it into my heart and life. In love and obedience I must appropriate the words of God and let them take full possession of my heart. Then they will indeed be words of life.

To secure a strong and powerful spiritual life, God's Word every day is indispensable. And if you seek fellowship with Him, you will find Him in His Word. Christ will teach you to commune with the Father through the Word, even as was His custom.

January 7

How to Read God's Word

"Blessed is the man whose delight is in the law of the Lord, and in His law doth he meditate day and night."
Psalm 1:1-2

Read God's Word with reverence. Let Him reveal His Word in your heart. *Read with careful attention.* How much higher are God's thoughts than our thoughts.

Read with the expectation of the guidance of God's Spirit. It is God's Spirit alone that can make the Word a living power in our hearts and lives. As you read, remember that God's Word and God's Spirit are inseparable. *Read with the firm purpose of keeping the Word day and night in your heart and in your life.* The whole heart and the whole life must come under the influence of the Word.

JANUARY 8

THE WORD AND PRAYER

"Quicken Me, O Lord, according to Thy Word."
Psalm 119:107

Prayer and the Word of God are inseparable and should always go together. *In His Word God speaks to me; in prayer I speak to God.* If there is to be true fellowship, God and I must both take part. What really gives prayer its power is that I take God's thoughts from His Word and present them before Him.

The Word teaches me how to pray – with strong desire, with a firm faith, and with constant perseverance. The Word teaches me not only what I am, but what I may become through God's grace. O Christian, learn this great lesson, *to renew your strength each day in God's Word, and so pray according to His will.*

JANUARY 9

OBEDIENCE

"Obey My voice ... and I will be your God."
Jeremiah 11:4

Pray God to imprint this lesson on your heart: *the life of faith is a life of obedience.* As Christ lived in obedience to the Father, so we too need obedience for a life in the love of God. Faith can firmly trust Christ to enable us to live such a life of love and of obedience.

Alas, the thought is too common: "I cannot be obedient, it is quite impossible." Yes, impossible to you, but not to God. He has promised "to cause you to walk in His statutes." Pray and meditate on these words, and the Holy Spirit will enlighten your eyes so that you will have power to do God's will.

January 10

Confession of Sin

"If we confess our sins, He is faithful and just to forgive us our sins, and to cleanse us from all unrighteousness."
1 John 1:9

Few Christians realize how necessary it is to be in earnest about an honest confession of sin or that it gives power to live the life of victory over sin. In fellowship with the Lord Jesus we need to confess with a sincere heart every sin that may be a hindrance in our Christian lives.

Confession means not only that I confess my sin with shame but that I hand it over to God, trusting Him to take it away. By an act of faith I reckon on God to deliver me. This deliverance means, in the first place, that I know my sins are forgiven, and secondly, that Christ undertakes to cleanse me from the sin and keep me from its power.

JANUARY 11

THE FIRST LOVE

"I have somewhat against thee,
because thou hast left thy first love."
Revelation 2:4

This is a thought of great significance – a church or a community or a Christian may be an example in every good work, and yet – *the tender love to the Lord Jesus in the inner chamber is missing.* Dear brother and sister, this book speaks of the fellowship of love with Christ in the inner chamber. Everything depends on this. Christ came from heaven to love us with the love wherewith the Father loved Him. He suffered and died to win our hearts for this love. *His love can be satisfied with nothing less than a deep, personal love on our part.*

JANUARY 12

THE HOLY SPIRIT

*"He shall glorify Me; for He shall
receive of Mine, and show it unto you."*
John 16:14

Our Lord, in the last night that He was with His disciples, promised to send the Holy Spirit as a Comforter. Although His bodily presence was removed, they would realize His presence in them and with them in a wonderful way.

When once we have grasped this truth, we will begin to feel our deep dependence on the Holy Spirit and pray the Father to send Him in power into our hearts. The Spirit will teach us to love the Word, to meditate on it, and to keep it. He will reveal the love of Christ to us, that we may love Him with a pure heart fervently.

JANUARY 13

CHRIST'S LOVE TO US

"Even as the Father hath loved Me,
I also have loved you: abide ye in My love."
John 15:9 RV

Of what value is abundance of riches if love is lacking between husband and wife or parents and children? And in our religion, of what value is all knowledge and zeal in God's work without the knowledge and experience of Christ's love? The one needful thing in the inner chamber is to know by experience *how much Christ loves you and to learn how you may abide and continue in that love.* He yearns that this everlasting love should rest upon us and work within us, that we may abide in it day by day. Do you realize that in your fellowship with Christ, in secret or in public, you are surrounded by and kept in this heavenly love?

JANUARY 14

OUR LOVE TO CHRIST

"Jesus Christ, whom not having seen, ye love: in whom though now ye see Him not, yet believing, … "
1 Peter 1:8 RV

What a wonderful description of the Christian life! People who had never seen Christ yet truly loved Him and believed on Him, so that their hearts were filled with unspeakable joy. Such is the life of Christians who really love their Lord.

This love is not merely a blessed feeling. It is an active principle. It takes pleasure in doing the will of the beloved Lord. It is a joy to keep His commandments. The love of Christ to us was shown by His death on the cross; our love must be exhibited in unselfish, self-sacrificing lives. *In the Christian life, love to Christ is everything!*

JANUARY 15

LOVE TO THE BRETHREN

"A new commandment I give unto you, that ye love one another, even as I have loved you, that ye also love one another."
John 13:34; 15:12

If we exhibit the love that was in God toward Christ and in Christ to us, the world will be obliged to confess that our Christianity is genuine and from above. Pray that you may love your fellow-believers with the same love with which Christ loved you. If we abide in Christ's love and let that love fill our hearts, supernatural power will be given to us to take all God's children unto our hearts in love. As close as is the bond of love between the Father and the Son, between Christ and His followers, so close must be the bond of love between all God's children.

JANUARY 16

LOVE TO SOULS

"Know that he which converteth a sinner from the error of this way, shall save a soul from death."
James 5:20

What a wonderful thought – that I may save a soul from everlasting death. If I convert him from the error of his ways. This is the calling not only of the minister, but of every Christian – to work for the salvation of sinners.

When Christ and His love took possession of our hearts, He gave us this love that we might bring others to Him. Let the reader examine himself and pray that in fellowship with Christ, he may think not only of his own soul but, having received the gift of God's love, he may pass it on to others. He will then know true happiness, the joy of bringing souls to Christ.

JANUARY 17

THE SPIRIT OF LOVE

"The love of God is shed abroad in our hearts,
by the Holy Spirit, which is given unto us."
Romans 5:5

We need continually to remind ourselves that it is not in our own strength or even by serious thought that we can attain to the love of Christ. It is only as we are wholly surrendered to the leading of the Spirit that we will be able to live according to God's will. Unless you wait upon God daily on your knees for His Spirit to be revealed in your heart, you cannot live in this love. Then you will indeed be rooted and grounded in love. A life of prayer will make a life in the love of Christ, in the love of one another, and in love to souls, a blessed reality in your experience.

January 18

Persevering Prayer

"Pray without ceasing."
1 Thessalonians 5:17

One of the greatest drawbacks to the life of prayer is the fact that the answer does not come as speedily as we expect. If we consider this matter we can see there may be a reason for the delay. Our desire must grow deeper and stronger, and we must ask with our whole heart.

"Pray without ceasing." You will find it an unspeakable blessing to do so. You will ask whether your prayer is really in accordance with the will of God and the Word of God. You will inquire if it is in the right spirit and in the Name of Christ. Keep on praying – you will learn that the delay in the answer to prayer is one of the most precious means of grace that God can bestow on you.

JANUARY 19

THE PRAYER MEETING

*"These all continued with one accord
in prayer and supplication."*
Acts 1:14

God's children meet together to lift up their hearts unitedly to God. By this means Christians are drawn closer to each other. Those who are weak are strengthened and encouraged by the more experienced members, and even young Christians have the opportunity of telling of the joy of the Lord. By means of intercession, God's blessing is poured out at home and abroad. You do not live for yourself alone but are part of the Body of Christ. As the roots of the tree hidden deep in the earth, and the branches spread out to heaven are one, so the hidden prayer life is inseparably bound up with united prayer.

JANUARY 20

INTERCESSION

"Praying at all seasons in the Spirit ... in all perseverance and supplication for all the saints."
Ephesians 6:18

What an unspeakable gift there is in intercession. That one should bring down blessings on others is an inconceivable honor. Should we not expect God's children to strive joyfully and with all their powers, by means of intercession, to bring down blessing on the world?

Christian, begin to use intercession as a means of grace for yourself and for others. If you surrender yourself to the guidance of the Holy Spirit and live a life wholly for God, you will realize that the time spent in prayer is an offering well-pleasing to God, bringing blessing to yourself and power into the lives of those for whom you pray.

JANUARY 21

PRAYER AND FASTING

"And Jesus said unto them, 'Because of your unbelief ...
this kind goeth not out but by prayer and fasting.'"
Matthew 17:20-21

Our Lord teaches us that a life of faith requires both prayer and fasting. Prayer grasps the power of heaven, fasting loosens the hold on earthly pleasure.

Let us learn that abstinence, temperance, and self-denial in temporal things are a help to the spiritual life. It helps to strengthen the soul for communion with God. To willingly sacrifice our own pleasure and to subdue the lust of the flesh and the lust of the eyes will help set our minds more fully on heavenly things. The very exertion needed in overcoming the desires of the flesh will give us strength to take hold of God in prayer.

JANUARY 22

THE SPIRIT OF PRAYER

"The Spirit maketh intercession for the saints."
Romans 8:27

I may bow in silence before God in the confidence that His Holy Spirit will teach me to pray. The Spirit is the Spirit of prayer. It is not my work but God's work in me. Our attitude should be one of silent expectation that as we pray, the Holy Spirit may help our infirmities and pray within us with groanings that cannot be uttered. Prayer is the work of the Triune God: the Father who wakens the desire and will give us all we need; the Son who through His intercession teaches us to pray in His Name; and the Holy Spirit who in secret will strengthen our feeble desires. The Spirit has been given from heaven to dwell in our hearts and to teach us to pray.

JANUARY 23

WHOLLY FOR CHRIST

*"One died for all ... that they which live should
no longer live unto themselves, but unto Him."*
2 Corinthians 5:14-15 RV

Happy the believer who realizes his high calling and the
privilege and blessedness of consecrating his life entirely
to God's service. Let nothing less be your earnest desire,
your prayer and your firm expectation: Christ has not only
died for me but lives in heaven to keep and sanctify me,
His purchased possession. Pray for grace to live wholly
for God in seeking souls and in serving His people. Take
time from day to day to be so united to Christ in the inner
man that you can say with all your heart: I live wholly
for Him who gave Himself wholly for me and now lives
in heaven wholly for me.

JANUARY 24

THE CROSS OF CHRIST

"I am crucified with Christ."
Galatians 2:20

The Christian shares with Christ in the cross. The crucified Christ lives in him through the Holy Spirit, and the spirit of the cross inspires him. He lives as one who has died with Christ. As he realizes the power of Christ's crucifixion, he lives as one who has died to the world and to sin.

Let the disposition of Christ on the cross, His humility, His sacrifice of all worldly honor, His spirit of self-denial take hold of you. The power of His death will work in you, and you will become like Him in His death, and you will know Him and the power of His resurrection.

JANUARY 25

THE WORLD

"Love not the world. If any man love the world, the love of the Father is not in him."
1 John 2:15

The world is that disposition or power under which man has fallen through sin. And the world still comes to us offering much to please the fleshly appetites. And much that the eye desires. And the pride of life, when a man imagines he knows and understands everything.

Christian, you live in a dangerous world. Cleave fast to the Lord Jesus. As He teaches you to shun the world and its attractions, your love will go out to Him in loyal-hearted service. But remember – There must be daily fellowship with Jesus. His love alone can expel the love of the world. Take time to be alone with your Lord.

January 26

Put on Christ

"Put ye on the Lord Jesus Christ, and make not provision for the flesh, to fulfill the lusts thereof."
Romans 13:14

We have put on the new man, and we have the new nature as a garment that is worn, by means of which all can see who we are. As I put on my clothes each day and am seen in them, so the Christian must put on the Lord Jesus, so that he no longer lives after the flesh to fulfill its lusts, but shows forth the image of his Lord and the new man formed in His likeness.

As my garments cover me and protect me, Christ Jesus will be my beauty, my defense, and my joy. As I commune with Him in prayer, He strengthens me to walk as one who is in Him and bound to Him forever.

JANUARY 27

THE STRENGTH OF THE CHRISTIAN

*"Finally, my brethren, be strong in the
Lord, and in the power of His might."*
Ephesians 6:10

The Christian needs strength. Where may strength be obtained? *The exceeding greatness of His power,* which raised Christ from the dead, *works in every believer.* We must pray that God, through His Spirit will teach us to believe in His almighty power.

Pray for God's Spirit to enlighten your eyes. Believe in the divine power working within you. Pray that the Holy Spirit may reveal it to you and appropriate the promise that God will manifest His Power in your heart, supplying all your needs.

JANUARY·28

THE WHOLE HEART

"With my whole heart have I sought Thee."
Psalm 119:10

When we want to make anything a success in worldly affairs, we put our whole heart into it. And is this not much more necessary in the service of a holy God? The whole heart is needed in the service of God when we worship Him in secret. And yet how little most Christians think of this. When we pray, and when we try to understand God's Word and to obey His commands, let us say: I desire to seek God, to serve Him, and to please Him, with my whole heart.

Think over it. Pray over it. Speak it out before God. Say it each morning as you approach God in prayer: I seek Thee with my whole heart.

JANUARY 29

IN CHRIST

"Of God are ye in Christ Jesus."
1 Corinthians 1:30

The Christian cannot read God's Word right nor experience its full power in his life until he prayerfully and believingly accepts this truth: *I am in Christ Jesus.*

Let our faith take hold of the words: "It is God that establisheth us in Christ." "Of God I am in Christ Jesus." The Holy Spirit will make it our experience. Pray earnestly and follow the leading of the Spirit. The word will take root in your heart, and you will realize something of its heavenly power. Abiding in Christ is a matter of the heart. It must be cultivated in a spirit of love. Only as we take time from day to day in fellowship with Christ will the abiding in Christ become a blessed reality.

JANUARY 30

CHRIST IN ME

"Know ye not ... that Jesus Christ is in you?"
2 Corinthians 13:5

What a difference it would make in our lives if we could take time every morning to be filled with the thought: Christ is in me. But this knowledge does not come easily. Through faith in God's Word, the Christian accepts it, and the Holy Spirit will lead us into all truth. Take time this very day to realize and appropriate this blessing in prayer.

Dear Christian, Paul said: "I bow my knees unto the Father." That is the only way to obtain the blessing. Take time in the inner chamber to realize: *Christ dwells in me.* Too little I have experienced this in the past, but I will cry to God and wait upon Him to perfect His work in me.

JANUARY 31

CHRIST IS ALL

"Christ is all and in all."
Colossians 3:11

In the eternal counsel of God, in the redemption on the cross, as King on the throne in heaven and on earth – *Christ is all!* In the salvation of sinners, in their justification and sanctification, *Christ is all!*

Do believe that if you will only accept the Lord Jesus in childlike faith you have a leader and a guide who will supply all your need. Let me take it as my motto – to teach me to pray, to strengthen my faith, to give me the assurance of His love and access to the Father, to make me strong for the work of the day: Christ is all. God be praised to all eternity: Christ, my Christ, is my all in all!

FEBRUARY

FEBRUARY 1

INTERCESSION

"Pray one for another."
James 5:16

What a mystery of glory there is in prayer! On the one hand, we see God, in His holiness and love and power, waiting, longing to bless man; and on the other, sinful man, bringing down from God by prayer the very life and love of heaven to dwell in his heart. But how much greater the glory of intercession! – when a man makes bold to say to God what he desires for others and seeks to bring down on one soul, or it may be on hundreds, the power of the eternal life with all its blessings. Would one not think that the Church would seek above everything to cultivate the power of an unceasing prayerfulness on behalf of the perishing world?

FEBRUARY 2

THE OPENING OF THE EYES

"And Elisha prayed and said: LORD,
open his eyes, that he may see ..."
2 Kings 6:17

The young man saw the mountain full of chariots of fire and horsemen about Elisha. How little the children of God live in the faith of that heavenly vision – the power of the Holy Spirit on them, with them, and in them for their own spiritual life and as their strength joyfully to witness for their Lord and His work! Let us pray especially that God may open all eyes to see what the great and fundamental need of the Church is in intercession to bring down His blessing, that the power of the Spirit may be known unceasingly in its Divine efficacy and blessing.

FEBRUARY 3

MAN'S PLACE IN GOD'S PLAN

"The heaven, even the heavens, are the LORD's;
but the earth hath He given to the children of men."
Psalm 115:16

The work God had begun and prepared for man was to be carried out in fulfillment of God's purpose. And so nature teaches us the wonderful partnership to which God calls man for the carrying out of the work of creation to its destined end. In this great redemption, God has revealed the power of the heavenly life and the spiritual blessings of which heaven is full. *But He has entrusted to His people the work of making these blessings known and making men partakers of them.* It is by the unceasing intercession of God's people that His Kingdom will come and His will be done on earth as it is in heaven.

FEBRUARY 4

INTERCESSION IN THE PLAN OF REDEMPTION

"O Thou that hears prayer, unto Thee shall all flesh come."
Psalm 65:2

When God made the plan of redemption, His object was to restore man to the place from which he had fallen. When Christ became man, it was that, as man, He might intercede for man. And He imparted this right of intercession to His disciples. God regards intercession as the highest expression of His people's readiness to receive and to yield themselves wholly to the working of His almighty power. It is only as God's children begin to see what intercession means in regard to God's Kingdom that they will realize how solemn their responsibility is.

FEBRUARY 5

GOD SEEKS INTERCESSORS

*"He saw that there was no man, and
wondered that there was no intercessor."*
Isaiah 59:16

Of what infinite importance is the place the intercessor holds in the Kingdom of God! God has willed that the working of His Spirit shall follow the prayer of His people. He waits for their intercession, showing where and how much of His Spirit they are ready to receive.

God rules the world and His Church through the prayers of His people. That God should have made the extension of His Kingdom to such a large extent dependent on the faithfulness of His people in prayer is a stupendous mystery. God calls for intercessors; in His grace He has made His work dependent on them; He waits for them.

FEBRUARY 6

CHRIST AS INTERCESSOR

"He is able to save them to the uttermost that come unto God by Him, seeing He ever liveth to make intercession for them."
Hebrews 7:25

In His life on earth Christ began His work as Intercessor. Think of His words to Peter, "I have prayed for thee, that thy faith fail not." Now that He is seated at God's right hand, He continues, as our great High Priest, the work of intercession without ceasing. But with this difference, *that He gives His people power to take part in it.* The power of heaven was to be at their disposal. The grace and power of God waited for man's bidding. Through the leading of the Holy Spirit, they would know what the will of God was. They would learn in faith to pray in His Name.

FEBRUARY 7

THE INTERCESSORS GOD SEEKS

"I have set watchmen upon thy walls, O Jerusalem; they shall never hold their peace day nor night: ye that are the LORD's remembrancers, take ye no rest and give Him no rest."
Isaiah 62:6-7

The great mark of the intercessors is to be that they are not to hold their peace day or night, to take no rest, and to give God no rest until the deliverance comes. In faith they may count upon the assurance that God will answer their prayer. If ever there was a time when God's elect should cry day and night to Him, it is now. Will you not, dear reader, offer yourself to God for this blessed work of intercession and learn to count it the highest privilege of your life to be a channel through whose prayers God's blessing can be brought down to earth?

FEBRUARY 8

THE SCHOOL OF INTERCESSION

"Who in the days of His flesh, when He had offered up prayers and supplications with strong crying and tears."
Hebrews 5:7

Let no one imagine it cost Christ nothing to become an intercessor. *The pouring out of the soul* – that is the Divine meaning of intercession. This giving of Himself over to live and die that He might save the perishing was a revelation of the spirit that has power to prevail with God.

Intercession must not be a passing interest; it must become an ever-growing object of intense desire for which above everything we long and live. It is the life of consecration and self-sacrifice that will indeed give power for intercession.

February 9

The Name of Jesus: The Power of Intercession

"Ask and ye shall receive, that your joy may be full."
John 16:24

When our Lord Jesus gave His unlimited prayer promise, He sent the disciples out into the world with this consciousness: "He who sits upon the throne and who lives in my heart has promised that what I ask in His name I shall receive. *He will do it.*" If Christians but knew what it is to yield themselves wholly and absolutely to Jesus Christ and His service, how their eyes would be opened to see that the power of all-prevailing intercession will indeed be the portion of those who live only in and for their Lord!

FEBRUARY 10

PRAYER: THE WORK
OF THE SPIRIT

*"God has sent forth the Spirit of His Son
into your hearts, crying, 'Abba, Father.'"*
Galatians 4:6

The Holy Spirit of Jesus is actually given into our hearts
that we may pray in His likeness, in His name, and in
His power. It is the Christian who is wholly yielded to
the leading of the Holy Spirit who will feel urged by the
compulsion of a Divine love to the undivided surrender
to a life of continual intercession, because he knows
that it is God who is working in him. It is the Holy Spirit
who breathes God's own desire into us and enables us
to intercede for souls.

FEBRUARY 11

JESUS CHRIST: OUR EXAMPLE IN INTERCESSION

*"He bare the sin of many and
made intercession for the transgressors."*
Isaiah 53:12

The Lord Jesus has in very deed taken us up into a partnership with Himself in carrying out the great work of intercession. He in heaven and we on earth must have one mind, one aim in life – that we should, from love to the Father and to the lost, consecrate our lives to intercession for God's blessing. The burning desire of the Father and Son for the salvation of souls must be the burning desire of our hearts too. And what a power for us to do the work because He pours forth His love into our hearts!

FEBRUARY 12

GOD'S WILL AND OURS

"Thy will be done."
Matthew 26:42

It is the high prerogative of God that everything in heaven and earth is to be done according to His will and as the fulfillment of His desires. When He made man in His image it was, above all, that his desires were to be in the likeness of God – that we are to feel and wish just as God. Man was to be the embodiment and fulfillment of God's desires. As in God so in man, desire is the great moving power. And just as man had yielded himself to a life of desire after the things of the earth and the flesh, God had to redeem him and to educate him into a life of harmony with Himself. His one aim was that man's desire should be in perfect accord with His own.

February 13

The Blessedness of a Life of Intercession

"Take ye no rest and give Him no rest, till He make Jerusalem a praise in the earth."
Isaiah 62:6-7

What blessedness, in union with other children of God, to strive until the victory is gained over difficulties here on earth or over the powers of darkness in high places! It is worth living for, to know that God will use me as an intercessor to receive and dispense His heavenly blessing and the power of His Holy Spirit. This is in very deed the life of heaven, the life of the Lord Jesus Himself in His self-denying love, taking possession of me and urging me to yield myself to bear the burden of souls before Him.

FEBRUARY 14

THE PLACE OF PRAYER

*"These all continued with one
accord in prayer and supplication."*
Acts 1:14

A Church of united and unceasing prayerfulness, a ministry filled with the Holy Spirit, the members living witnesses to a living Christ with a message to every creature on earth – such was the Church that Christ founded and such the Church that went out to conquer the world.

Their own duty was to wait in united and unceasing prayer for the power of the Holy Spirit as the gift from on high for their witness to Christ to the ends of the earth. A praying Church, a Spirit-filled Church, a witnessing Church with all the world as its sphere and aim – such is the Church of Jesus Christ.

FEBRUARY 15

PAUL AS AN INTERCESSOR

"I bow my knees unto the Father, that He would grant
you to be strengthened with might by His Spirit."
Ephesians 3:14, 16

We do not sufficiently think of Paul as the Intercessor who sought and obtained, by his supplication, the power that rested upon all his other activities and brought down the blessing that rested on the churches that he served.

The whole relationship between pastor and people is a heavenly one, spiritual and Divine, and can only be maintained by unceasing prayer. It is when ministers and people waken up to the consciousness that the power and blessing of the Holy Spirit is waiting for their united and unceasing prayer that the Church will begin to know something of what Christianity is.

FEBRUARY 16

INTERCESSION FOR LABORERS

*"Pray ye therefore the Lord of the harvest, that
He will send forth laborers into His harvest."*
Matthew 9:37-38

Christ meant to teach us that however large the field
may be and however few the laborers, prayer is the
best, the sure, the only means for supplying the need.
It is not only in time of need that the prayer must be
sent up, but the whole work is to be carried on in the
spirit of prayer. To meet the need of the world, its open
fields and its waiting souls, the churches all complain
of the lack of laborers and of funds. Does not Christ's
voice call us to the united and unceasing prayer of the
first disciples? God is faithful by the power of His Spirit
to supply every need.

FEBRUARY 17

INTERCESSION FOR INDIVIDUAL SOULS

"Ye shall be gathered one by one."
Isaiah 27:12

Oh, when will Christians learn the great truth that "what God in heaven desires to do *needs prayer on earth as its indispensable condition.*" It is as we realize this that we shall see that intercession is the chief element in the conversion of souls. All our efforts are vain without the power of the Holy Spirit given in answer to prayer. Let every Christian make a beginning in the exercise of intercession on behalf of single individuals. God wants every redeemed child of His to intercede for the perishing. It is the vital breath of the normal Christian life.

FEBRUARY 18

INTERCESSION FOR MINISTERS

"Finally, brethren, pray for us."
2 Thessalonians 3:1

If Paul, after having preached for twenty years in the power of God, still needed the prayer of the Church, how much more does the ministry in our day need it? The minister needs the prayer of his people. He has a right to it. It is his task to train Christians for their work of intercession on behalf of the Church and the world. He must begin with training them to pray for himself. Let all intercessors who are seeking to enter more deeply into their blessed work give a larger place to the ministry, whether of their own church or of other churches. Let them continue in prayer and watch therein, that ministers may be full of power, full of prayer, and full of the Holy Spirit.

FEBRUARY 19

PRAYER FOR ALL SAINTS

*"With all prayer and supplication praying
at all seasons in the Spirit, for all the saints."*
Ephesians 6:18

The great lack in true believers often is that in prayer they are occupied with themselves and with what God must do for them. It is as we forget ourselves, in the faith that God will take charge of us, and yield ourselves to the great and blessed work of calling down the blessing of God on our brothers and sisters, that the whole church will be fitted to do its work in making Christ known to every creature. This alone is the healthy and the blessed life of a child of God who is wholly yielded to Christ Jesus.

FEBRUARY 20

MISSIONARY INTERCESSION

*"When they had fasted and prayed, and laid
their hands on them, they sent them away."*
Acts 13:3

Missions have their root in the love of Christ that was
proved on the cross and now lives in our hearts. As
men are so earnest in seeking to carry out God's plans
for the natural world, so God's children should be at
least as wholehearted in seeking to bring Christ's love
to everyone. Intercession is the chief means appointed
by God to bring the great redemption within the reach
of all. Pray for the missionaries, that the Christ-life may
be clear and strong, that they may be people of prayer
and filled with love in whom the power of the spiritual
life is made manifest.

FEBRUARY 21

THE GRACE OF INTERCESSION

"Continue in prayer, and watch in the same with thanksgiving, withal praying also for us."
Colossians 4:2-3

O my brothers and sisters, how little we realize what we are losing in not living in fervent intercession! What may we not gain for ourselves and for the world if we allow God's Spirit, as a Spirit of grace and supplication, to master our whole being. There is nothing that can bring us nearer to God and lead us deeper into His love than the work of intercession.

God delights in nothing so much as in prayer. Shall we not learn to believe that the highest blessings of heaven will be unfolded to us as we pray more?

FEBRUARY 22

UNITED INTERCESSION

"There is one body, and one Spirit."
Ephesians 4:4

It is only when intercession *for the whole Church, by the whole Church* ascends to God's throne that the Spirit of unity and of power can have its full sway. Let us bless God that there is a unity in Christ Jesus, deeper and stronger than any visible manifestations could make it. *It is in the cultivation and increase of the Spirit and in the exercise of intercession that the true unity can be realized.* As believers are taught what is the meaning of their calling as a royal priesthood, they are led to see that God is not confined in His love or promises to their limited spheres of labor, but invites them to enlarge their hearts and to pray for all who believe.

FEBRUARY 23

UNCEASING INTERCESSION

"Pray without ceasing."
1 Thessalonians 5:17

"Pray without ceasing". Who can do it? To the true believer it holds out the promise of the highest happiness, of a life crowned by all the blessings that can be brought down on souls through his intercession. And as he perseveres, it becomes increasingly his highest aim upon earth, his highest joy, his highest experience of the wonderful fellowship with the holy God.

Let us take that word as a promise of what God's Spirit will work in us. How close and intimate our union and likeness to the Lord Jesus can be. Let it become one of the chief elements of our heavenly calling.

February 24

Intercession: The Link Between Heaven and Earth

"Thy will be done, as in heaven, so on earth."
Luke 11:2

The intercession of the Son begun upon earth, continued in heaven, and carried on by His people upon earth, will bring about mighty change. Every prayer of a parent for a child, of a believer for the saving of the lost, or for more grace to those who have been saved is part of the great unceasing cry going up day and night from this earth, "As in heaven, so on earth."

Child of God, will you not yield yourself, like Christ, to live with this one prayer: "Father, Thy will be done on earth as in heaven"?

FEBRUARY 25

GOD'S DESIRES

"Here will I dwell; for I have desired it."
Psalm 132:13-14

Here you have the one great desire of God that moved Him in the work of redemption. His heart longed for man, to dwell with him and in him. As the desire of God toward us fills our hearts, it will waken within us the desire to gather others around us to become His dwelling too. I can pray to God for those around me, to give them His Holy Spirt. It is God's great plan that man himself shall build Him a habitation. It is in answer to the unceasing intercession of His children that God will give His power and His blessing. And shall we not give our lives for the fulfillment of His heart's desire?

FEBRUARY 26

MAN'S DESIRE

*"Delight thyself in the LORD; and He
shall give thee the desires of thine heart."*
Psalm 37:4

"Delight thyself in the Lord," and in His life of love, "and
He will give thee the desires of thine heart." We may be
sure that, as we delight in what God delights in, such
prayer is inspired by God and will have its answer. In
fellowship with Him we gain courage and confidence that
our prayers for the persons in which we are interested
will be heard. As we reach out in yearning love, we shall
get the power to take hold of the will of God to bless and
believe that God will work out His own blessed will in
giving us the desires of our hearts, because the fulfillment
of His desire has been the delight of our souls.

FEBRUARY 27

MY GREAT DESIRE

"That I may dwell in the house
of the Lord all the days of my life."
Psalm 27:4

Here we have man's response to God's desire to dwell in us. When the desire of God toward us begins to rule the life and heart, our desire is fixed on one thing and that is to dwell in the house of the Lord all the days of our life, to behold the beauty of the Lord, to worship Him in the beauty of holiness. The more we realize the desire of God's love to give His rest in the heart and the more our desire is thus quickened to dwell every day in His temple and behold His beauty, the more the Spirit of intercession will grow upon us to claim all that in His new covenant God has promised.

FEBRUARY 28

INTERCESSION DAY AND NIGHT

> *"Shall not God avenge His own elect,*
> *which cry day and night unto Him."*
> Luke 18:7

Is such prayer night and day really needed and really possible? Most assuredly, when the heart is first so entirely possessed by the desire that it cannot rest until this is fulfilled. The life has so come under the power of the heavenly blessing that nothing can keep it from sacrificing all to obtain it.

God grant that our hearts may be so brought under the influence of these Divine truths that we may in very deed yield ourselves to make our devotion to Christ and our longing to satisfy the heart of God the chief object of our life.

THE HIGH PRIEST AND HIS INTERCESSION

"He ever liveth to make intercession for them."
Hebrews 7:25

Our great High Priest alone has power with God, in a never-ceasing intercession, to obtain from the Father what His people need. The blessing that He obtains from His Father for us, He holds for His people to receive from Him through their fervent supplication to be dispensed to the souls among whom He has placed them as His witnesses and representatives. When Christians realize that salvation means a vital life union with Jesus Christ, the Church will prove how truly the likeness and power of Christ dwell in her.

MARCH

MARCH 1

A ROYAL PRIESTHOOD

*"Call unto Me, and I will answer thee, and show thee
great and mighty things which thou knowest not."*
Jeremiah 33:3

Children of God, God counts upon you to take your place
before His throne as intercessors. Awake, I pray you, to the
consciousness of your holy calling as a royal priesthood.
Is this asking too much – to yield your life for this holy
service of the royal priesthood to that blessed Lord who
gave Himself for us?

As you plead for the great mercies of the new covenant
to be bestowed, take with you this thought: The infinite
willingness of God to bless. He delights in mercy. He
waits to be gracious.

MARCH 2

INTERCESSION: A DIVINE REALITY

*"And another angel came, ... and there was
given unto him much incense, that
he should offer it with the prayers of all saints."*
Revelation 8:3

Intercession is an essential element in God's redeeming
purpose. Christ's intercession in heaven is essential to
His carrying out of the work He began upon earth, but He
calls for the intercession of the saints in the attainment
of His object. As the reconciliation was dependent on
Christ's doing His part, so in the accomplishment of the
work, He calls on the Church to do her part. Intercession
is a Divine reality. Without it, the Church loses one of its
chief beauties, loses the joy and the power of the Spirit
life for achieving great things for God.

MARCH 3

TRUE WORSHIP

"Worship God."
Revelation 22:9

We must give God time to make Himself known to us.
Believe with your whole heart that just as you present
yourself to God as a supplicant, *so God presents Himself
to you as the Hearer of prayer.* But you cannot realize
this except as you give Him time and quiet. He Himself
will give the assurance that in His time your prayer will
be heard.

To seek Him, to find Him, to tarry in His presence, to
be assured that He actually listens to what we say and is
working in us – it is this that gives the inspiration that
makes prayer as natural as the conversation of a child
with his father.

MARCH 4

GOD IS SPIRIT

"God is Spirit: ... worship Him in spirit and in truth."
John 4:24

God is Spirit, most holy and most glorious. He gave us a spirit with the one object of *holding fellowship with Himself*. Through sin that power has been darkened and well-nigh quenched. There is no way for its restoration but by presenting the soul in stillness before God for the working of His Holy Spirit in our spirit. Deeper than our thoughts and feelings, God will in our spirits within us, teach us to worship Him in spirit and in truth. "The Father seeketh such to worship Him." He Himself by the Holy Spirit will teach us this if we wait upon Him. In this quiet hour, be still before God and yield yourself with your whole heart to believe in and to receive the gentle working of His Spirit.

MARCH 5

INTERCESSION AND ADORATION

"Worship the LORD in the beauty of holiness."
Psalm 96:9

The better we know God the more wonderful becomes our insight into the power of intercession. We begin to understand that it is the great means by which man can take part in the carrying out of God's purpose.

Intercession will lead to the feeling of the need of a deeper adoration. Adoration will give new power for intercession. A true intercession and a deeper adoration will ever be found to be inseparable. The secret of true adoration can only be known by the soul that gives time to tarry in God's presence and that yields itself to God. "Oh, come let us worship and bow down, let us kneel before the Lord our Maker."

MARCH 6

THE DESIRE FOR GOD

"With my soul have I desired Thee in the night."
Isaiah 26:9

What is the chief thing, the greatest and most glorious, that one can see or find upon earth? *Nothing less than God Himself.* And what is the chief and the best and the most glorious thing that one needs every day and can do every day? Nothing less than to seek and to know and to love and to praise this glorious God. As glorious as God is, so is the glory which begins to work in the hearts and lives of those who give themselves to live for God. Have you learned what is the first and greatest thing you have to do every day? To seek God, to meet Him, to worship Him, to live for Him and for His glory.

MARCH 7

SILENT ADORATION

*"My soul is silent unto God ... for
my expectation is from Him."*
Psalm 62:1, 5

When we in our littleness and God in His glory meet, we understand that what God says has infinitely more worth than what we say. And yet our prayer so often consists in the utterance *of our thoughts* that we give God no time to speak to us. Our prayers are often so indefinite and vague. Let us remember the promise, "In quietness and confidence shall be your strength." Such worship of God – in which you bow low in your nothingness and lift up your thoughts to realize God's presence – is the sure way to give Him the glory that is His due. It opens the way to fellowship with Him.

MARCH 8

THE LIGHT OF GOD'S COUNTENANCE

"The Lord is my light."
Psalm 27:1

Every morning the light of God shines upon His children. But in order to enjoy the light of God's countenance, the soul must turn to God and trust Him to let His light shine upon it. Believe that it is the ardent longing of your Father that you should dwell and rejoice in His light all the day. In the midst of difficulties, the light of God will rest upon you without ceasing. *Make sure that the light of God shines upon you in the morning,* and you can count upon the light being with you all the day.

MARCH 9

FAITH IN GOD

"Jesus said unto them: 'Have faith in God.'"
Mark 11:22

Faith is the power by which we see the light of God and walk in it. We were made for God, to seek Him, to find Him, to grow up into His likeness and show forth His glory. And faith is the eye which, turning away from the world and self, looks up to God and in His light sees light. To faith God reveals Himself.

Let our one desire be to take time and be still before God, believing with an unbounded faith in His longing to make Himself known to us. Let us feed on God's Word to make us strong in faith. Let that faith have large thoughts of what God's glory is; of what His longing love is to get complete possession of us.

MARCH 10

ALONE WITH GOD

"And it came to pass, as He was alone praying."
Luke 9:18

We need to be alone with God, to yield to the presence and the power of His holiness, of His life, and of His love. Christ on earth needed it; He could not live the life of a Son here in the flesh without at times separating Himself entirely from His surroundings and being alone with God. How much more must this be indispensable to us! Alone with God – that is the secret of true prayer, of true power in prayer; of real living, face-to-face fellowship with God; and of power for service. "There is no path to holiness, but in being *much and long alone with God.*" Take time, O my soul, to be alone with God.

MARCH 11

WHOLLY FOR GOD

"There is none upon earth that I desire beside Thee."
Psalm 73:25

Alone with God – This is a word of the deepest importance. May we seek grace from God to reach its depths. Then shall we learn that there is another word of equally deep significance – *Wholly for God.*

Nature teaches us that if anyone desires to do a great work, he must give wholly to it. And shall we not think it reasonable that the great God of Love should have us wholly for Himself? Shall we not take the watchword, "Wholly for God," as the keynote for our devotions every morning? *As wholly as God gives Himself to us, so wholly He desires that we give ourselves to Him.*

MARCH 12

THE KNOWLEDGE OF GOD

"This is life eternal, that they might know Thee."
John 17:3

The knowledge of God is absolutely necessary for the spiritual life. *It is life eternal.* Not the intellectual knowledge we receive from others or through our own power of thought, but the living, experimental knowledge *in which God makes Himself known to the soul.* Just as the rays of the sun on a cold winter's day warm the body, imparting its heat to us, *so the living God sheds the life-giving rays of His holiness and love into the heart that waits Him.* One of the very first things in prayer is to be silent before God, that He may reveal Himself. By His hidden but mighty power, God will manifest His presence, resting on us and working in us.

MARCH 13

GOD THE FATHER

*"Baptizing in the name of the Father,
and of the Son, and of the Holy Spirit."*
Matthew 28:19

When Christ taught us to say, "Our Father, which art in heaven," He immediately added, "Hallowed be Thy Name." As God is holy, so we are to be holy too. And there is no way of becoming holy but by counting that name most holy and drawing nigh to Him in prayer. How often we speak that name without any sense of the unspeakable privilege of our relation to God. If we would just take time to worship Him in His Father love, how the inner chamber would become to us the gate of heaven.

MARCH 14

GOD THE SON

*"Grace to you and peace from God our
Father and the Lord Jesus Christ."*
Romans 1:7

It may cause spiritual loss if we do not grasp the truth
that it is only through faith in Christ and *in living union
with Him* that we can enjoy a full and abiding fellowship
with God. If you would know and worship God aright,
seek Him and worship Him *in Christ.* And if you seek
Christ, seek Him and worship Him *in God.*

Take time to meditate and believe, to expect all from
God the Father who sits upon the throne and from the
Lord Jesus Christ, the Lamb in the midst of the throne.
Then you will learn truly to worship God.

MARCH 15

GOD THE HOLY SPIRIT

"Through Him we both have access
by one Spirit unto the Father."
Ephesians 2:18

In our communion with God in the inner chamber, we must guard against the danger of seeking to know God and Christ in the power of the intellect or the emotions. *The Holy Spirit has been given for the express purpose that "by Him we may have access to the Father through the Son."*

Be strong in the faith that He is working secretly in you and give yourself wholly to His guidance. We must believe that the "greater works" of the Spirit for the enlightening and strengthening of the spiritual life – the fullness of the Spirit – will be given in answer to prayer.

MARCH 16

THE SECRET OF THE LORD

*"Enter into thy closet, and when
thou hast shut thy door, pray."*
Matthew 6:6

Christ longed greatly that His disciples should know God as their Father and that they should have secret fellowship with Him. In His own life He found it not only indispensable but the highest happiness to meet the Father in secret. And He would have us realize that it is impossible to be true, whole-hearted disciples *without daily communion with the Father in heaven.* God would draw us away from the world and from ourselves. He offers us, instead, the blessedness of close, intimate communion with Himself. We should day by day confidently seek the renewal of our spiritual life in prayer to the Father who is in secret.

MARCH 17

HALF AN HOUR OF SILENCE IN HEAVEN

"And there was silence in heaven about the space of half an hour."
Revelation 8:1

God longs to bless you. Is it not worth the trouble to take half an hour alone with God? If you persevere, you may find that the half-hour that seems the most difficult in the whole day may at length become the most blessed in your whole life.

Read some passage of Scripture and let God's Word speak to you. Then bow in deepest humility before God and wait on Him. He will work with you. Begin to pray. Keep on, though the time may seem long. God will reward you.

MARCH 18

GOD'S GREATNESS

*"Thou art great, and doest wondrous
things; Thou art God alone."*
Psalm 86:10

When we commence an important work, we take time
to consider the greatness of the undertaking. The right
comprehension of God's greatness will take time. But if we
give God the honor that is His due and if our faith grows
strong in the knowledge of what a great and powerful
God we have, we shall be drawn to tarry in the inner
chamber to bow in humble worship before this great and
mighty God. Meditate on Psalm 45:3, 6-7 until you are
filled with some sense of what a glorious Being God is.
Take time for these words to master the heart until you
bow in adoration before God.

MARCH 19

A PERFECT HEART

"For the eyes of the LORD run to and fro in behalf
of them whose heart is perfect toward Him."
2 Chronicles 16:9

It is absolutely necessary to seek God with a perfect heart – for Christians to give themselves to God's service with all the power of their will. What an encouragement this should be to us to humbly wait upon God with an upright heart; we may be assured that His eye will be upon us and will show forth His mighty power in us and in our work.

O Christian, have you learned this lesson in your worship of God – to yield yourself each morning with your whole heart to do God's will? Pray each prayer with a perfect heart, in true whole-hearted devotion to Him.

MARCH 20

THE OMNIPOTENCE OF GOD

"I am the Almighty God."
Genesis 17:1

When Abraham heard these words, he fell on his face; and God spoke to him. O Christian, have you bowed in deep humility before God until you felt that you were in living contact with the Almighty, until your heart has been filled with the faith that the Almighty God is working in you and will perfect His work in you?

Do you wonder that many Christians complain of weakness and shortcomings? They do not understand that the Almighty God must work in them every hour of the day. When we fully believe that the mighty power of God is working without ceasing within us, we can joyfully say, "God is the strength of my life."

MARCH 21

THE FEAR OF GOD

"Blessed is the man that feareth the Lord."
Psalm 112:1

The fear of God – these words characterize the religion of the Old Testament and the foundation which it laid for the more abundant life of the New. We need texts such as the one at the top of the page fully expounded and young converts fully instructed in the need and the blessedness of a deep fear of God leading to an unceasing prayerfulness as one of the essential elements of the life of faith. "The gift of holy fear" is ever still the great desire of the child of God and an essential part of a life that is to make a real impression on the world.

MARCH 22

GOD INCOMPREHENSIBLE

"Behold, God is great, and we know Him not."
Job 36:26

It is of the utmost importance to feel deeply that God's ways are infinitely exalted beyond all our thought.

His Greatness – Incomprehensible.
His Might – Incomprehensible.
His Omnipresence – Incomprehensible.
His Wisdom – Incomprehensible.
His Holiness – Incomprehensible.
His Mercy – Incomprehensible.
His Love – Incomprehensible.

As we worship, let us cry out: What an inconceivable glory is in this Great Being who is my God and Father!

MARCH 23

THE HOLINESS OF GOD (OT)

"Be holy, for I am holy."
Leviticus 11:45; 19:2; 20:7-8; 21:8, 15, 23; 22:9, 16

Nine times these words are repeated in Leviticus. Israel had to learn that as holiness is the highest and most glorious attribute of God, so it must be the marked characteristic of His people. He that would know God aright must above all desire to be holy as He is holy.

Child of God, if you would meet your Father in secret, bow low and worship Him in the glory of His holiness. Give Him time to make Himself known to you. Be still, and take time to worship God in His great glory and in that deep condescension in which He longs and offers to dwell with us and in us. *"Worship the Lord in the beauty of holiness."*

MARCH 24

THE HOLINESS OF GOD (NT)

"Holy Father, keep through Thine own name those whom Thou hast given Me. Sanctify them."
John 17:11

Ponder deeply these words as you read them and use them as a prayer to God: "Blessed Lord, strengthen my heart to be unblameable in holiness. God Himself sanctify me wholly. God is faithful, who also will do it." What a privilege to commune with God in secret, to speak these words in prayer, and then to wait upon Him until through the working of the Spirit, they live in our hearts, and we begin to know something of the holiness of God.

God's holiness has been revealed in the Old Testament. In the New, we find the holiness of God's people in Christ through the sanctification of the Spirit.

MARCH 25

SIN

"The chief of sinners. And the grace of our Lord was exceeding abundant with faith and love which is in Christ Jesus."
1 Timothy 1:14

Never forget that it is sin that has led to the great transaction between you and Christ Jesus and that each day in your fellowship with God, His one aim is to deliver and keep you fully from its power and lift you up into His likeness and His infinite love. It is the thought of sin ever surrounding you and seeking to tempt you, that will keep you low at His feet and give the deep undertone to all your adoration; that will give fervency to your prayer and urgency to the faith that hides itself in Christ.

MARCH 26

THE MERCY OF GOD

"Oh, give thanks unto the LORD; for He is good: for His mercy endureth forever."
Psalm 136:1

This Psalm is wholly devoted to the praise of God's mercy. In each of the twenty-six verses we have the expression: "His mercy endureth forever." Our hearts too should be filled with the blessed assurance. The everlasting, unchanging mercy of God is cause for unceasing praise and thanksgiving. Of all God's other attributes, mercy is the crown. May it be a crown upon my head and in my life!

O my soul, how frequently we have read these familiar words without the least thought of their immeasurable greatness! Be still and meditate until the heart responds.

MARCH 27

THE WORD OF GOD

"The Word of God is quick and powerful."
Hebrews 4:12

The Word teaches me to know the God to whom I pray. The Word comes from God's heart and brings His thoughts and His love into my heart.

The Word teaches me God's will – the will of His promises as to what He will do for me as food for my faith; His commands to which I surrender myself in loving obedience. *"God's Word in deepest reverence in our hearts and on our lips and in our lives will be a never-failing fountain of strength and blessing."* I believe that God's Word is indeed full of a quickening power that will make me strong. Above all, it will give me the daily blessed fellowship with Him as the living God.

MARCH 28

THE PSALMS

"How sweet are Thy words unto my taste!
yea, sweeter than honey to my mouth!"
Psalm 119:103

Would you each morning truly meet God and worship Him in spirit and in truth, *then let your heart be filled with the Word of God in the Psalms.* As you read the Psalms, underline the word "Lord" or "God", wherever it occurs, and also the pronouns referring to God, "I", "Thou", "He". This will help to connect the contents of the Psalm with God, who is the object of all prayer. These underlined words will make God the central thought and lead you into a new worship of Him. Take them upon your lips and speak them out before Him. Your faith will anew be strengthened to realize how God is your strength.

MARCH 29

THE GLORY OF GOD

"Unto Him be glory throughout all ages."
Ephesians 3:21

God Himself must reveal His glory to us; then alone are we able to know and glorify Him aright. What a lesson for the soul that longs to see the glory of God in His Word. Put aside your own efforts and thoughts. Let your heart be as a photographic plate that waits for God's glory to be revealed. The plate must be rightly prepared and clean; let your heart be prepared and purified by God's Spirit. If you keep silence before God and give Him time, He will put thoughts into your heart that may be of unspeakable blessing to yourself and others. He will create within you desires and dispositions that will indeed be as the rays of His glory shining in you.

MARCH 30

THE HOLY TRINITY

"Elect according to God the Father,
the Spirit and Jesus Christ."
1 Peter 1:2

We must remind ourselves that, for all our communion with God, the presence and the power of the Son and the Spirit are absolutely necessary. Have you not often felt it a mockery to speak of five minutes to be alone with God? And now does not the thought of the true worship of God in Christ through the Holy Spirit make you feel more than ever that it needs time to enter into such holy alliance with God as shall keep the heart and mind all day in His peace and presence? *It is in tarrying in the secret of God's presence that you receive grace to abide in Christ and all the day to be led by His Spirit.*

MARCH 31

THE LOVE OF GOD

*"God is love; and he that dwelleth
in love dwelleth in God, and God in him."*
1 John 4:16

The best and most wonderful word in heaven is Love. For God is Love. And the best and most wonderful word in the inner chamber must be – Love. For the God who meets us there is Love. Love finds its joy in imparting all that it has to make the loved one happy. And the heavenly Father has no other object than to fill our hearts with His love. All the other attributes of God find in this their highest glory. The true and full blessing of the inner chamber is nothing less than a life in the abundant love of God. Take time in silence to meditate on the wonderful revelation of God's love in Christ.

APRIL

APRIL 1

WAITING UPON GOD

"On Thee do I wait all the day."
Psalm 25:5

Waiting upon God – in this expression we find one of the deepest truths of God's Word in regard to the attitude of the soul in its communion with God. Just think – that He may reveal Himself in us; teach us all His will; do to us what He has promised; that in all things He may be the Infinite God. It is the attitude of the soul with which each day should begin. In everything there should be a waiting upon God to receive what He will bestow, to see what He will do, to allow Him to be the Almighty God.

The deep root of all Scriptural theology is this: Absolute dependence on God.

APRIL 2

THE PRAISE OF GOD

"Praise is comely for the upright."
Psalm 33:1

Praise will ever be a part of Adoration. Adoration, when it has entered God's presence and had fellowship with Him, will ever lead to the praise of His name. Let praise be a part of the incense we bring before God in our quiet time. In the Psalms we see what a large place praise ought to have in the spiritual life. Let us take time to study this until our whole heart and life are one continual song of praise: *"I will bless the Lord at all times; His praise shall continually be in my mouth"; "I will sing praises unto my God while I have my being."* Let our prayer be that we may offer to God ever a heart filled with unceasing praise.

APRIL 3

THE IMAGE OF GOD

*"And God said, 'Let us make man
in our image, after our likeness.'"*
Genesis 1:26

God undertook the stupendous work of making a creature, who is not God, to be a perfect likeness of Him in His Divine glory. Man was to live in entire dependence on God and to receive directly and unceasingly from Himself the inflow of all that was holy and blessed in the Divine Being. God's glory, His holiness, and His love were to dwell in him and shine out through him. Let us keep the heart set upon the glory of the image of God in Christ in the assurance that the Spirit will change us into the same image day by day.

APRIL 4

THE OBEDIENCE OF FAITH

"I am God Almighty: walk before Me, and be thou perfect.'"
Genesis 17:1

Children of Abraham, children of God, the Father makes great demands on your faith. If you are to follow in Abraham's footsteps, you too are to forsake all to live in the land of spiritual promise with nothing but His word to depend upon, separated unto God. For this you will need a deep and clear insight that the God who is working in you is the Almighty who will work all His good pleasure. Do not think that it is easy to live the life of faith. It needs a life that seeks to abide in His presence all the day. Bow before God in humble worship until He speaks to you. There you have the secret birthplace of the power to trust God for everything that He promises.

APRIL 5

THE LOVE OF GOD

*"Thou shalt love the LORD thy God with all thine heart,
and with all thy soul, and with all thy might."*
Deuteronomy 6:5

This was the first commandment as the origin and fountain out of which the others naturally proceed. It has its grounds in the relationship between God as the loving Creator and man made in His image as the object of that love.

This perfect heart, loving God with all our might, is what God claims, is what God is infinitely worthy of, is what God *will Himself give and work in us.* Let our whole soul go out in faith to meet, to wait for, and to expect the fulfillment of the promise – to love God with the whole heart is what God Himself will work in us.

APRIL 6

THE JOYFUL SOUND

"Blessed is the people that know the joyful sound."
Psalm 89:15-16

"Glad tidings of great joy," was what the angel calls the Gospel message. This is what is here spoken of as "the joyful sound." That blessedness consists in God's people walking in the light of God and rejoicing in His name all the day. Undisturbed fellowship, everlasting joy is their portion. It is the heritage of all who are seeking to love God with all their heart and with all their strength. The deeper we seek to enter into God's will for us, the stronger will the assurance come that what the Father has meant for us will be wrought through Christ.

APRIL 7

THE THOUGHTS OF GOD

"So are My thoughts higher than your thoughts."
Isaiah 55:9

We need daily, tender, abiding fellowship with God if we are to enter into His mind and have His thoughts make their home in us. And what a faith is needed to believe that God will not only reveal the beauty and glory of these thoughts, but will so mightily work in us that their Divine reality and blessing shall fill our inmost being.

What deep reverence and humility and patience we need in waiting upon God by His Holy Spirit to impart to our hearts the life and the light that can make us feel at home with these thoughts. Christ promised that the Spirit would glorify Him, would fill us with the light of the heavenly world.

APRIL 8

THE NEW COVENANT IN JEREMIAH

"I will make a new covenant with the house of Israel."
Jeremiah 31:31

God promises to make a new covenant in which provision would be made to enable men to live a life of obedience. This promise ensures a continual, whole-hearted obedience as the mark of the believer who takes God at His Word. God's mighty power will be shown in the heart of everyone who believes the promise: *"They shall not depart from Me"; "It shall be even so as it hath been spoken unto Me."* Bow in deep stillness before God and believe what He says. The definite promise of the New Testament is the fruit of heart renewal and the power of the Holy Spirit leading the soul and revealing the fullness of grace to keep us "unblameable in holiness."

APRIL 9

THE NEW COVENANT IN EZEKIEL

"And I will put My Spirit within you,
and cause you to walk in My statutes."
Ezekiel 36:27

The great mark of the new covenant would be a Divine power enabling them to walk in His statutes. The requirement of the law is fulfilled in all who walk in the Spirit. Just one thing is needed – the faith in an omnipotent God who will by His wonderful power do what He has promised.

Oh, let us begin to believe that the promise will come true. Let us believe all that God here promises, and God will do it. To an extent beyond all power of thought, God has made His great and glorious promises dependent on our faith!

APRIL 10

THE NEW COVENANT AND PRAYER

"Call unto Me, and I will answer thee, and will shew thee great things, and difficult, which thou knowest not."
Jeremiah 33:3 RV

The fulfillment of the great promises of the new covenant is made dependent on prayer. It is when individual men and women turn to God with their whole heart to plead these promises that He will fulfill them. It is in the exercise of intense persevering prayer that faith will be strengthened to take hold of God and surrender itself to His omnipotent working. As Christians testify of what God has done, believers will help each other and take their place as the Church of the living God, pleading for, and fully, expecting that His promises will be fulfilled in larger measure.

APRIL 11

THE NEW COVENANT IN HEBREWS

"For I will be merciful to their iniquities,
and their sins will I remember no more."
Hebrews 8:12

Jesus Christ is "the Mediator of the new covenant," with the forgiveness of sin in the power of His blood and the Law written in the heart in the power of His Spirit. Oh that we could understand that just as surely as the complete pardon of sin is assured, the complete fulfillment of the promises may be expected too. It needs strong, whole-hearted desire for a life wholly given up to Him. It means a surrender to Jesus Christ as the Mediator of the new covenant, a willingness to accept our place with Him, crucified to the world and to sin and to self. It means a readiness to follow Him at any cost.

117

APRIL 12

THE TRIAL OF FAITH

*"If the prophet had bid thee do some great
thing, wouldst thou not have done it?"*
2 Kings 5:13

In Naaman we have a striking Old Testament illustration
of the place faith takes in God's dealing with us. Think
first of how intense Naaman's desire was for healing. In
this seeking for God and His blessing we have the root of
a strong faith which is too much lacking in our religion.
The second mark of faith is that it has to give up all its
preconceived opinions and to bow before the Word of
God. Faith is often held back by the thought how such
a simple thing as to accept God's Word can effect such
a mighty revolution of the heart. Then comes the third
mark: faith proves itself in obedience.

APRIL 13

FAITH IN CHRIST

"Ye believe in God, believe also in Me."
John 14:1

Dear Christians, do you not see of what deep importance it is that you take time to worship Jesus in His Divine Omnipotence as one with the Father? That will teach you to count on Him in His sufficiency to work in us all that we can desire. This faith must so possess us that every thought of Christ will be filled with the consciousness of His presence as an Almighty Redeemer, able to save and sanctify and empower us to the very uttermost.

The deity of Christ is the rock upon which our faith depends. As the Almighty God, Christ will work for you and in you and through you all that God desires and all that you can need.

APRIL 14

CHRIST'S LIFE IN US

"Because I live, ye shall live also."
John 14:19

Alas, how many there are who are content with the beginnings of the Christian life but never long to have it in its fullness, the more abundant life! They are not ready for the sacrifice implied in being wholly filled with the life of Jesus. I pray you, do take time, and let Christ's wonderful promise take possession of your heart. Be content with nothing less than a full salvation, *Christ living in you, and you living in Christ.* The disciples were to receive from Him the resurrection life in the power of its victory over death and of His exaltation to the right hand of God. He would from thenceforth ever dwell in them; a new, a heavenly, an eternal life – the life of Jesus Himself – should fill them. And this promise is to all who will accept it in faith.

APRIL 15

THE OBEDIENCE OF LOVE

"If ye keep My commandments, ye shall abide in My love."
John 15:10

How can I come to abide in Christ always? To live wholly for Him? The Lord gives the simple but far-reaching answer: "Keep My commandments." This is the only, the sure, the blessed way of abiding in Him. "If ye keep My commandments, ye shall abide in My love; even as I have kept My Father's commandments and abide in His love." Loving obedience is the way to the enjoyment of His love. The wonderful promise of the Holy Spirit as the power of Christ's life in them was the pledge that they would indeed love Him and keep His words. This was to be the great secret of abiding in Christ, of having the indwelling of Christ, and of the Divine efficacy of prayer.

APRIL 16

THE PROMISE OF THE SPIRIT

"If I go away, the Comforter will come unto you."
John 16:7

It is this Spirit of God and of Christ that the Church lacks so sadly; it is this Spirit she grieves so unceasingly. It is owing to this that her work is so often feeble and fruitless. And what can be the reason of this? The Spirit is God. We have thought too much of Him as our help in the Christian life; we have not known that heart and life are to be entirely and unceasingly under His control; we are to be led by the Spirit every day and every hour. In His power our life is to be a direct and continual abiding in the love and fellowship of Jesus. The Spirit that searches the deep things of God claims the very depths of our being, there to reveal Christ as Lord and Ruler.

APRIL 17

IN CHRIST

"In that day ye shall know that I am
in My Father, and ye in Me, and I in you."
John 14:20

The secret of the believer's power is to be found in nothing less than where Christ found it, abiding in the Father and His love. The Divine life of heaven, of Christ in God and God in Christ, is the picture and the pledge of what our life in Christ is to be here upon earth.

Blessed Lord, we beseech Thee, teach us to surrender ourselves unreservedly to the Holy Spirit and so daily above everything to wait for His teaching, that we too may know the blessed secret, that *as Thou art in the Father and the Father worketh through Thee, so we are in Thee, and Thou workest through us.*

APRIL 18

ABIDING IN CHRIST

"Abide in Me, and I in you."
John 15:4

The great need is to take time in waiting on the Lord Jesus in the power of His Spirit, until the two great truths get the complete mastery of your being. As Christ is in God – this is the testimony from heaven; as the branch is in the vine – this is the testimony of all nature. "He that abideth in Me, bringeth forth much fruit." Fruit, more fruit, much fruit is what Christ seeks, is what He works, is what He will assuredly give to the soul that trusts Him. To one and all the message comes: daily, continuous, unbroken abiding in Christ Jesus is the one condition of a life of power and of blessing. Take time and let the Holy Spirit so renew in you the secret abiding in Him.

APRIL 19

THE POWER OF PRAYER

"Ask whatsoever ye will, and it shall be done unto you."
John 15:7 RV

Before our Lord went to heaven He taught His disciples two great lessons in regard to their relation to Him in the great work they had to do. The one was that in Heaven He would have much more power than He had upon earth and that He would use that power for the salvation of men, solely through them, their word and their work. The other was that they without Him could do nothing, but that they could count upon Him to work in them and through them and so carry out His purpose. Their first and chief work would therefore be to bring everything they wanted done to Him in prayer.

APRIL 20

THE MYSTERY OF LOVE

*"I pray that they may all be one; even
as Thou, Father, art in Me, and I in Thee."*
John 17:21

The power to convince the world that God loved the
disciples as He loved His Son could only come as
believers lived out their life of having Christ in them and
proving it by loving their brethren as Christ loved them.
The feebleness of the Church is owing to this – that our
life in Christ and His life in us is not known and not
proved to the world by the living unity in which our love
manifests that Christ is in us. Nothing less than this is
needed: such an indwelling of Christ in the heart, such
a binding together of believers because they know and
see and love each other.

APRIL 21

CHRIST OUR RIGHTEOUSNESS

*"Justified freely by His grace through
the redemption that is in Christ Jesus."*
Romans 3:24

Justification comes at the commencement full and complete, as the eye of faith is fixed upon Christ. But that is only the beginning. Gradually believers begin to understand that they were at the same time born again, *that they have Christ in them, and that their calling now is to abide in Christ, and let Christ abide and live and work in them.* The Christian life must be "from faith to faith". The grace of pardon is but the beginning; growing in grace leads on to fuller insight and experience of what it is to be in Christ, to live in Him, and to grow up in Him in all things as the Head.

APRIL 22

CHRIST OUR LIFE

*"Reckon ye also yourselves to be dead unto
sin, but alive unto God in Christ Jesus."*
Romans 6:11 RV

Just as the new life in us is an actual participation in
and experience of the risen life of Christ, so our death to
sin in Christ is also an actual spiritual reality. It is when,
by the power of the Holy Spirit, we are enabled to see
how really we were one with Christ on the cross in His
death and in His resurrection, that we shall understand
that in Him sin has no power over us. Those who know
that they died in Christ and now are alive in Him can
confidently count upon the word, "sin shall not have
dominion over you," not even for a single moment. The
power of Christ is living in them for a life of holiness
and fruitfulness.

APRIL 23

CRUCIFIED WITH CHRIST

*"I have been crucified with Christ; yet I live;
and yet no longer I, but Christ liveth in me."*
Galatians 2:20

In Christ we are made partakers of a death to sin and into the will and the life of God. Such was the death Christ died; such is the death we are made partakers of in Him. To Paul this was such a reality that he was able to say: "I have been crucified with Christ" This death had such power that he no longer lived his own life; Christ lived His life in him. Christ's death on the cross was His highest exhibition of His holiness and His victory over sin. And the believer who receives Christ is made partaker of all the power and blessing that the crucified Lord has won.

APRIL 24

THE FAITH LIFE

*"That life which I now live in the flesh, I live
in faith, the faith which is in the Son of
God, who loved me and gave Himself up for me."*
Galatians 2:20 RV

If we ask Paul what he meant by saying that he no longer
lives but that Christ lives in him, what now is his part in
living that life? He gives us the answer: His whole life,
day by day and all the day, was an unceasing faith in the
wonderful love that had given itself for him. Faith was
the power that possessed and permeated his whole being
and his every action. It is a faith which has got a vision
of how entirely Christ gives Himself to the soul to be, in
the very deepest sense of the word, His life.

April 25

Full Consecration

*"I count all things to be loss for the excellency
of the knowledge of Christ Jesus my Lord."*
Philippians 3:8

To count all things but loss for Christ was the keynote of Paul's life, as it must be that of ours if we are to share fully in the power of His resurrection. How little the Church understands that we have been entirely redeemed from the world, to live wholly and only for God and His love. Christ claims the whole heart and the whole life and the whole strength, if we are indeed to share with Him in the victory through the power of the Holy Spirit. Christ calls us to walk every day in the closest union with Himself, to abide in Him without ceasing, and so to live as those who are wholly His.

APRIL 26

ENTIRE SANCTIFICATION

"And the God of peace Himself sanctify you wholly;
Faithful is He that calleth you, who will also do it."
1 Thessalonians 5:23-24 RV

What a promise! One would expect to see all God's children clinging to it, claiming its fulfillment. Just listen. God, the God of peace – keeping our hearts and thoughts in Christ Jesus – can and will do it. This God of peace Himself promises to sanctify us wholly in Christ our sanctification, in the sanctification of the Spirit. It is God who is doing the work. It is in close personal fellowship with God Himself that we become holy. He will do it; and He will give me grace so to abide in His nearness that I can ever be under the cover of His perfect peace and of the holiness which He alone can give.

APRIL 27

THE EXCEEDING
GREATNESS OF HIS POWER

*"That ye may know what is the exceeding
greatness of His power to us-ward who believe."*
Ephesians 1:17-19 RV

What a mighty working of the power of God, to raise
Christ out of the grave to the power and the glory of His
throne. And now it is that very same power we are to
know as working in us every day. It is by that Almighty
power that the risen and exalted Christ can be revealed
in our hearts as our life and our strength. Oh, let us trust
God for His Holy Spirit to enable us to claim nothing less
every day that the exceeding greatness of this resurrection
power.

APRIL 28

THE INDWELLING CHRIST

"That Christ may dwell in your heart by faith."
Ephesians 3:14-19

The great privilege that separated Israel from other nations was this: they had God dwelling in their midst, His Home in the Holiest of all, in the tabernacle and the temple. The New Testament is the dispensation of the indwelling God in the Heart of His people. The Gospel – the dispensation of the indwelling Christ.

It is in the very nature of Christ, in His Divine omni-presence and love, to long for the heart to dwell in. As faith sees this and bows the knee and pleads with God for this great blessing, it receives grace to believe that the prayer is answered and in that faith accepts the wonderful gift – Christ dwelling in the heart by faith.

APRIL 29

CHRISTIAN PERFECTION

"The God of peace make you perfect in every good
work to do His will, working in you that which
is well-pleasing in His sight, through Jesus Christ."
Hebrews 13:20-21

The great thought here is that all that Christ had wrought out for our redemption and all that God had done in raising Him from the dead was just with the one object that He might now have free scope for working out in us that everlasting redemption which Christ had brought in. He Himself as God the Omnipotent will make us perfect in every good work. I have just one thing to do, to yield myself into God's hands for Him to work. Not to hinder Him by my working, but to be assured that He will work in me all that is well-pleasing in His sight.

APRIL 30

THE GOD OF ALL GRACE

"The God of all grace, who called you unto His eternal glory in Christ, shall Himself perfect, stablish, strengthen you, after ye have suffered a little while."
1 Peter 5:10

Just as God is the center of the universe, the one source of its strength, the one Guide that orders and controls its movements, so God must have the same place in the life of the believer. With every new day the first and chief thought ought to be – God, God alone, can fit me this day to live as He would have me. And what is not to be our position toward God? The first thought of every day ought to be the humble placing of ourselves in His hands to yield ourselves to receive from Him the fulfillment of His promises.

MAY

MAY 1

NOT SINNING

"Ye know that He was manifested to take away sins; and in Him is no sin. Whosoever abideth in Him sinneth not."
1 John 3:5-6

Though there is sin in our nature, the abiding in Christ, in whom is no sin, does indeed free us from the power of sin and enables us day by day to live so as to please God.

As I seek to abide in Him in whom there is no sin, Christ will indeed live out His own life in me in the power of the Holy Spirit and fit me for a life in which I always do the things that are pleasing in His sight. The promise is sure: God the Almighty has pledged that He will work in you what is well-pleasing in His sight through Christ Jesus. In that faith, abide in Him.

MAY 2

OVERCOMING THE WORLD

"Who is he that overcometh the world, but he
that believeth that Jesus is the Son of God?"
1 John 5:5

The world still exerts a terrible influence over the Christian who does not know that in Christ he has been crucified to the world. In the pleasure in eating and drinking, in the love and enjoyment of what there is to be seen of its glory, and in all that constitutes the pride of life, the power of this world proves itself. And most Christians are either utterly ignorant of the danger of a worldly spirit or feel themselves utterly powerless to conquer it. As the child of God abides in Christ and seeks to live the heavenly life in the power of the Holy Spirit, he may confidently count on the power to overcome the world.

May 3

Jesus: The Author and Perfector of Our Faith

"Lord, I believe; help Thou mine unbelief."
Mark 9:24

Here we receive the assurance that the Christ is a Savior *who Himself will care for our faith*. Even though it be but as a mustard seed; in contact with Christ the feeblest faith is made strong and bold. Jesus Christ is the Author and Perfector of our faith. Take the hidden feeble seed of the little faith you have with the Word of promise on which you are resting; plant it in your heart. Give utterance to it in contact with Jesus Christ and fervent prayer to Him. A feeble faith in the Almighty Christ will become the great faith that can remove mountains.

MAY 4

THE LOST SECRET

*"Ye shall be baptized with the
Holy Spirit not many days hence."*
Acts 1:5

The Church appears to have lost possession of that which ought to be to her a secret of secrets – the abiding consciousness, that it is only as she lives in the power of the Holy Spirit that she can preach the Gospel in demonstration of the Spirit and of power. It is owing to this that there is so much preaching and working with so little of spiritual result, and especially that there is so little of that much-availing prayer that brings down the Power from on high on her ministrations. Let us seek earnestly the grace of the Holy Spirit, who alone can Himself reveal to us the things which God loves to do for them that wait upon Him.

MAY 5

THE KINGDOM OF GOD

"Jesus showed Himself to His disciples ... speaking of the things pertaining to the Kingdom of God."
Acts 1:3

In the last command our Lord gave to His disciples (Acts 1:4, 8) we find the great essential characteristics of the Kingdom of God in great power.

1. The King – the crucified Christ.
2. The disciples – His faithful followers.
3. The power for their service – the Holy Spirit.
4. Their work – testifying for Christ as His witnesses.
5. Their aim – the ends of the earth.
6. Their first duty – waiting on God in united, unceasing prayer.

MAY 6

CHRIST AS KING

"'There be some of them which stand here, which shall not taste of death, till they have seen the Kingdom of God.'"
Mark 9:1

The mark of what a kingdom is, is to be seen in *the King*. Christ now reigns as God and Man on the throne of the Father. On earth, its power is seen in the lives of those in whom it rules.

We must know that Christ actually as King dwells and rules in our hearts. We must know that we live in Him and in His power are able to accomplish all that He would have us do. Our whole life is to be devoted to our King and the service of His Kingdom. This blessed relationship to Christ means above all daily fellowship with Him in prayer.

MAY 7

JESUS THE CRUCIFIED

*"God hath made that same Jesus, whom
ye have crucified, both Lord and Christ."*
Acts 2:36

This our King is the crucified Jesus. Christ's cross is His
highest glory. It is through this that He has conquered
every enemy and gained His place on the throne of God.
Each one of us needs to experience fellowship with Christ
in His cross if the Spirit of Pentecost is really to take
possession of us. It is as we become "conformable to His
death", in the entire surrender of our will, in the entire
self-denial of our old nature, in the entire separation from
the spirit of this world, that we can become the worthy
servants of a crucified King.

MAY 8

THE APOSTLES

"He charged them to wait for the promise of the Father."
Acts 1:4 RV

The second mark of the Church is to be found in *the disciples* whom the Lord had prepared to receive His Spirit and to be His witnesses.

Let this be the test by which we try ourselves whether we have indeed surrendered to the fellowship of Christ's sufferings and death, hated our own life and crucified it – and received the power of Christ's life in us. This will give us liberty to believe that God will hear our prayer too and give us His Holy Spirit to work in us what we and He desire, if we are indeed with one accord to take up the disciples' prayer and to share in the answer.

May 9

NOT OF THIS WORLD

*"They are not of the world even
as I am not of the world."*
John 17:14, 16

One great mark of the disciples was to be that as little as Christ was of the world, so little were they to be of the world. Christ and they had become united in the cross and the resurrection; they both belonged to the Kingdom of heaven. This separation from the world is to be the mark of all disciples who long to be filled with the Spirit.

Let each one who would take up the Pentecostal prayer for the power of the Holy Spirit examine himself whether the spirit of this world is not that secret of that lack of love of prayer which is absolutely necessary in all who would plead the promise of the Spirit.

MAY 10

OBEDIENCE

*"If ye love Me, ye will keep my commandments ...
and He shall give you another Comforter."*
John 14:15-16

For the true Christian, Christ is all. Each one who prays
for the power of the Spirit must be ready to say: "I yield
myself with my whole heart this day to the leading of the
Spirit"; a full surrender is the question of life or death,
an absolute necessity.

The surrender to live every day, all the day, abiding in
Christ and keeping His commandments is to be the one
mark of your discipleship. It is when the child of God
learns that it is only as the heart longs in everything to do
God's will that the Father's love and Spirit can rest upon
it. This will be the secret of power in our intercession.

MAY 11

THE HOLY SPIRIT

*"Ye shall receive power when the
Holy Spirit is come upon you."*
Acts 1:8

It is only when Christ had, by His death, broken the power of sin and won in the resurrection a new life for all to live in Himself, that the Spirit of God could come and take possession of the whole heart and make it a dwelling place for God. Nothing less than this could be the power in us by which sin could be overcome and the prisoners set free. The Spirit reveals Christ in us as our life and our strength for a perfect obedience and the preaching of the Word in the power of God. Amazing mystery! The Spirit of God, our life; the Spirit of Christ, our light and strength.

MAY 12

THE POWER FROM ON HIGH

"Tarry ye until ye be clothed with power from on high."
Luke 24:49

The Holy Spirit would possess the disciples, and their work would be in very deed the work of the Almighty Christ. Their whole posture each day would be that of unceasing dependence, prayer and confident expectation. They had indeed learned to know Christ intimately. And they had not only seen Him but known Him in the power of His resurrection and the experience of that resurrection lived in their own hearts.

Everything calls the Gospel minister to rest content with nothing less than the indwelling life and power of the Holy Spirit revealing Jesus in the heart as the only fitness for preaching the Gospel in power.

MAY 13

MY WITNESSES

"Ye shall be My Witnesses."

Acts 1:8

Christ's servants are to be witnesses to Him, ever testifying of His wonderful love, of His power to redeem, of His continual abiding presence, and of His wonderful power to work in them.

This is the only weapon that the King allows His redeemed ones to use. Without claiming authority or power, without wisdom or eloquence, without influence or position, each one is called, not only by his words but by his life and action, to be a living *proof and witness of what Jesus can do.* Here we have the secret of a flourishing Church: *every believer is a witness for Jesus.*

May 14

The Gospel Ministry

*"The Spirit of truth, He shall testify
of Me, and ye shall also bear witness."*
John 15:26-27

This is the high calling and also the only power of the preacher of the Gospel – in everything to be *a witness for Jesus.* He may never forget that it is for this especially that he has been set apart, to be with the Holy Spirit a witness for Christ. It is as he does this that sinners will find salvation, that God's children will be sanctified and fitted for His service.

This teaching must ever be a personal testimony from the experience to what Christ is and can do. It is this that will build up believers so that they can walk in such fellowship with Jesus Christ that He can reveal Himself through them.

MAY 15

THE WHOLE WORLD

"My witnesses unto the uttermost parts of the earth."
Acts 1:8

The words that Christ spoke to His disciples gives them the assurance that the Holy Spirit would maintain in them Christ's divine power. In the strength of that promise the Church can make the ends of the earth its aim. Oh, that Christian people might understand that the extension of God's Kingdom can only be affected by the united continued prayer of men and women who give their hearts wholly to wait upon Christ in the assurance that what they desire He will do for them. Oh, that God would grant that His children proved their faith in Christ by making His aim their aim and yielding themselves to be His witnesses in united, persevering prayer.

MAY 16

THE WHOLE EARTH FILLED WITH HIS GLORY

"Let the whole earth be filled with His glory."
Psalm 72:19

What a prospect! This earth now under the power of the Evil One renewed and *filled with the glory of God* – a new earth wherein righteousness dwells.

This great work of bringing the knowledge of Christ to every creature has been entrusted to the Church. His power and His faithfulness are pledges that one day we shall see the whole earth filled with the glory of God. What blessedness to know that prayer will indeed help and be answered!

MAY 17

THE FIRST PRAYER MEETING

*"These all with one accord continued
steadfastly in prayer, with the women."*
Acts 1:14

It is difficult to form a right conception of the unspeakable importance of this first prayer meeting in the history of the Kingdom. It was to be for all time the indication of the one condition on which His Presence and Spirit would be known in Power. In it we have the secret key that opens the storehouse of heaven with all its blessings. Where Christ's disciples are linked to each other in love and yield themselves wholly to Him in undivided consecration, the Spirit will be given from heaven as the seal of God's approval, and Christ will show His mighty power.

MAY 18

THE UNITY OF THE SPIRIT

"Endeavoring to keep the unity of
the Spirit. There is one body and one Spirit."
Ephesians 4:3-4

There is a very great need that the children of God throughout the world should be drawn together in the consciousness of their being chosen by God to be a holy priesthood, ministering continually the sacrifice of praise and prayer. Let none of us think it too much to give a quarter of an hour every day for meditation on some word of God connected with His promises to His Church – and then to plead with Him for its fulfillment. Slowly, unobservedly, and yet surely, you will taste the blessedness of being one, heart and soul, with God's people and receive the power to pray the effectual prayer that availeth much.

MAY 19

UNION IS STRENGTH

"When they had prayed, they were all filled with the Holy Spirit. And the multitude were of one heart."
Acts 4:31-32

The power of union we see everywhere in nature. How feeble is a drop of rain, but many drops united in one stream is an irresistible power. Such is the power of true union in prayer. Let us believe that when in the Spirit God's people reach out their hands to each other, there will be power to resist the terrible influence that the world can exert. And in that unity God's children will have power to prevail with God. It is in the fellowship of loving and believing prayer that our hearts can be melted into one and we shall become strong in faith to believe what God has promised.

MAY 20

PRAYER IN THE NAME OF CHRIST

"Whatsoever ye shall ask in My Name, that will I do."
John 14:13

Christ longs to rouse a large and confident faith and to free our prayer from every shadow of a doubt and to teach us to look upon intercession as the most certain and most blessed way of bringing glory to God, joy to our own souls and blessing to the perishing world around us. *It was when the Holy Spirit came that they would have power thus to pray.* It is to draw us on to yield ourselves fully to the Spirit that He holds out the precious promise, "Ask and ye shall receive, that your joy may be full." As we believe in the power of the Spirit working in us in full measure, intercession will become to us the joy and strength of all our service.

May 21

Your Heavenly Father

"Our Father which art in heaven."
Luke 11:2

How simple, how beautiful, this invocation which Christ puts upon our lips! And yet how inconceivably rich in meaning, in the fullness of the love and blessing it contains. What a gift Christ bestowed on us when He gave us the right to say: "Father!" We count it a great privilege as we bow in worship to know that the Father comes near to us where we are upon earth. But we soon begin to feel the need of rising up to enter into His Holy Presence in heaven, to breathe its atmosphere, to drink in its spirit, and to become truly heavenly-minded. And as we enter the Holiest of all, the word "heavenly Father" gets a new meaning.

May 22

The Power of Prayer

*"The effectual fervent prayer of a
righteous man availeth much."*
James 5:16

Prayer availeth much. It avails much with God. It avails much in the history of His church and people. Prayer is the one great power which the Church can exercise in securing the working of God's omnipotence in the world.

"The *effectual fervent prayer* of a righteous man availeth much." It is only when the righteous man stirs up himself and rouses his whole being to take hold of God that the prayer availeth much. As Jacob said: "I will not let thee go"; as the importunate widow gave the just Judge no rest, so it is that the effectual fervent prayer effects great things.

May 23

Prayer and Sacrifice

"I would that ye knew what great conflict I have for you."
Colossians 2:1

Christians need to prepare themselves to pray, "with their whole heart and strength." The secret of powerful prayer is sacrifice of ease, of time, of self.

Prayer is sacrifice. Our prayer has its worth alone from being rooted in the sacrifice of Jesus Christ. Need we wonder at the lack of power in our prayer where there is so much reluctance to make the needful sacrifice in waiting upon God. Christ, the Christ we trust in, the Christ that lives in us offered Himself a sacrifice to God. It is as this spirit lives and rules in us that we shall receive power from Him as intercessors to pray the effectual prayer that availeth much.

MAY 24

THE INTERCESSION OF THE SPIRIT FOR THE SAINTS

"He maketh intercession for the saints according to the will of God."
Romans 8:27

Where and how does the Spirit make intercession for the saints? In the heart which knows not what to pray, He secretly and effectually prays what is according to the Will of God. This implies that we trust Him to do His work in us and that we tarry before God even when we know what to pray, in the assurance that the Holy Spirit is praying in us. This implies further that we exercise an unbounded dependence upon the Holy Spirit even when we have nothing to offer but groanings and sighs.

MAY 25

THAT THEY ALL MAY BE ONE

*"Holy Father, keep them in Thy Name
that they may be one, even as we are."*
John 17:11

"That they may be one" – The Lord longs that these
words and the thought shall have the same place in our
hearts that they have in His. How little the church has
understood this. Shall we not welcome heartily the prayer
"that they may be one" a chief part of our daily fellowship
with God? How simple it would be when once we
connected the two words "Our Father," with all the children of God throughout the world. We should make these
words part of our unceasing intercession. That will enable
us to fulfill the new commandment that we should love
the brethren as He loved us that our joy might be full.

MAY 26

THE DISCIPLES' PRAYER

"They continued steadfastly in fellowship and in prayers."
Acts 2:42

What a lesson it would be to us to have a clear apprehension of what continuing with one accord in prayer meant for the disciples. However defective the thoughts were that they had of the Blessed Spirit, this they knew, from the words of Jesus, "it is expedient for you that I go away," that the Spirit would give the glorified Christ into their very hearts in a way they had never known Him before. And it would be He Himself, in the mighty power of God's Spirit, who would be their strength for the work to which He had called them. With what confidence they expected the fulfillment of the promise. And with what intensity and persistency they pleaded.

MAY 27

PAUL'S CALL TO PRAYER

"Praying at all seasons in the Spirit."
Ephesians 6:18 RV

What a sense Paul had of the deep divine unity of the whole body of Christ and of the need for unceasing prayer for all the members of it. He expects believers to be so filled with the consciousness of their being in Christ and through Him united consciously to the whole body, that their highest aim would ever be the welfare of the body of Christ. He counted on their being filled with the Spirit so that it would be perfectly natural to them to pray for all who belong to the Body of Christ. Is not this what we need in our daily life, that every believer who is yielded undividedly to Christ Jesus shall live in the consciousness of oneness with Christ and His body?

MAY 28

PAUL'S REQUEST FOR PRAYER

"That I may open my mouth boldly, to
make known the mystery of the Gospel."
Ephesians 6:19-20

Paul had now been a minister of the Gospel for more than twenty years. One would say that it would come naturally to him to speak boldly. But so deep is his conviction of his own insufficiency and weakness, so absolute is his dependence on Divine teaching and power, that he feels that without the direct help of God he cannot do the work as it ought to be done. The sense of his total and unalterable dependence upon God who was with him, teaching him what and how to speak, is the ground of all his confidence and the keynote of his whole life.

MAY 29

PRAYER FOR ALL SAINTS

"To the Saints and faithful brethren in Christ,
We give thanks to God, praying always for you."
Colossians 1:1-4

Prayer for all saints: let this be our first thought. It will need time and thought and love to realize what is included in that simple expression. Think of your own neighborhood and the saints you know; of your whole country and praise God for all who are His saints; of all Christian nations of the world and the saints to be found in each of these; of all the heathen nations and the saints of God to be found among them in ever-increasing numbers.

MAY 30

PRAYER BY ALL SAINTS

*"We trust in God that He will yet deliver us;
you also helping together by prayer for us."*
2 Corinthians 1:10-11

It may be that in time believers will stand together in helping to rouse those around them to take heart in the great work that the prayer *for all saints* may become *one by all saints.*

This message is sent out like radio waves to all who desire to be in touch with it and to seek to prove their consecration to their Lord in the unceasing daily supplication for the power of His love and Spirit to be revealed to all His people.

MAY 31

PRAYER FOR ALL THE FULLNESS OF THE SPIRIT

"Prove me now therewith, saith the LORD of Hosts,
if I will not pour you out a blessing."
Malachi 3:10

The only remedy for inefficiency to enable us to gain the victory over the powers of this world or of darkness is in the manifested presence of our Lord in the midst of His hosts and in the power of His Spirit. As we connect the prayer for the whole Church on earth with the prayer for the whole power of God in heaven, we shall feel that the greatest truths of the heavenly world have possession of us and that we are asking what God is longing to give, as soon as He finds hearts utterly yielded to Him.

JUNE

June 1

Every Day

"Give us day by day our daily bread."
Luke 11:3

Surely if the children of God themselves once yielded themselves with their whole lives to God's love and service, they should count it a privilege to avail themselves of any invitation that would help them *every day* to come into God's Presence with the great need of His Church and Kingdom. Are there not many who confess that they desire to live wholly for God? They welcome every opportunity for proving that they are devoting their heart's strength to the interests of Christ's Kingdom and to the prayer that can bring down God's blessing.

JUNE 2

WITH ONE ACCORD

*"They were all with one accord in one place
and they were all filled with the Holy Spirit."*

Acts 2:1, 4

We may indeed thank God, for we know of tens of thousands of His children who in daily prayers, are pleading for some portion of the work of God's Kingdom. The power of each individual member is increased to a large degree by the inspiration of fellowship with a large and conquering host. Nothing can so help us to an ever-larger faith as the consciousness of being one body and one spirit in Christ Jesus. It was as the disciples were all with one accord in one place in the Day of Pentecost that they were all filled with the Holy Spirit. May we ever be mindful that united prayer brings the answer to prayer.

JUNE 3

A PERSONAL CALL

"We trust not in ourselves, but in God who delivered us."
2 Corinthians 1:9-10

When we plead with Christians to pray without ceasing, there are a very large number who quietly decide that such a life is not possible for them. And yet it is to such that we bring the call to offer themselves for a whole-hearted surrender to live entirely for Christ. We come to them with the assurance that God can change their lives and fill their hearts with Christ and His Holy Spirit. They need to listen to the call for men and women who will every day live in the spirit of unceasing intercession for all saints, that they receive the power of the Holy Spirit and acknowledge that this is nothing less than a duty, a sacrifice that Christ's love has a right to claim.

June 4

The Redemption of the Cross

"Christ redeemed us."
Galatians 3:13

The cross reveals to us man's sin as under a curse, Christ becoming a curse and so overcoming it, and our full and everlasting deliverance from the curse. The lost and most hopeless sinner finds a sure ground of confidence and of hope. Such is the Gospel of God's love – the penitent sinner can now rejoice that the curse is put away forever. The preaching of the redemption of the cross is the foundation and center of the salvation the Gospel brings us. There is nothing which will keep the heart more tender toward God, enabling us to live in His love and make Him known to those who have never yet found Him. God be praised for the redemption of the cross.

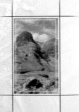

JUNE 5

THE FELLOWSHIP OF THE CROSS

"Have this mind in you, which was also in Christ Jesus."
Philippians 2:5

Paul here tells us what that mind was in Christ: He emptied Himself; He took the form of a servant; He humbled Himself, even to the death of the cross. It is this deep humility that gave up His life to death, that is to be the spirit that animates us. It is thus that we shall prove and enjoy the blessed fellowship of His cross. Each would bear in his life the marks of the cross with its sentence of death on the flesh, with its entire denial of self, with its growing conformity to the crucified Redeemer in His deep humility and entire surrender of His will to the life of God. It is no easy school and no hurried learning – this school of the cross.

JUNE 6

CRUCIFIED WITH CHRIST

"I have been crucified with Christ; yet I live;
and yet no longer I, but Christ liveth in me."
Galatians 2:20

The thought of fellowship with Christ in His bearing the cross has often led to the vain attempt in our own power to follow Him and bear His image. But this is impossible until we know the meaning of, "I have been crucified with Christ." The power of His death and life work in me. The life that I have received from Him is a life that has been crucified and made free from the power of sin. As faith realizes that I no longer live but Christ lives in me as the Crucified one, life in the fellowship of the cross becomes a possibility and a blessed experience.

JUNE 7

CRUCIFIED TO THE WORLD

"Far be it from me to glory, save in the cross of our Lord Jesus Christ, through which the world hath been crucified unto me, and I unto the world."
Galatians 6:14

When Paul said: "I have been crucified with Christ," it was not only an inner spiritual truth, but an actual, practical experience in relation to the world and its temptations. It was this that made him glory in the cross of Christ.

When the world crucified Christ, it crucified you with Him. When Christ overcame the world on the cross, He made you an overcomer too. He calls you now, at whatever cost of self-denial, to regard the world in its hostility to God and His Kingdom as a crucified enemy over whom the cross can ever keep you conqueror.

JUNE 8

THE FLESH CRUCIFIED

*"They that are in Christ Jesus have crucified the
flesh with the passions and the lusts thereof."*
Galatians 5:24

Those who are Christ's and have accepted Him as the
Crucified One little understand what that includes. Alas,
how many there are who have never for a moment thought
of such a thing! It may be that the truth of our being
crucified with Christ has not been taught. They shrink
back from the self-denial that it implies, and as a result,
where the flesh is allowed in any measure to have its way,
the Spirit of Christ cannot exert His power. The Spirit can
alone guide us in living faith and fellowship with Christ
Jesus as the flesh is kept in the place of crucifixion.

JUNE 9

BEARING THE CROSS

"He that doth not take his cross and follow after Me, is not worthy of Me. He that loseth his life for My sake shall find it."
Matthew 10:38-39

Christ would have His disciples understand that their nature was so evil and corrupt that it was only in losing their natural life that they could find the true life. Christ asks of His disciples that they should forsake all and take up their cross, give up their whole will and life, and follow Him. The call comes to us to give up the self life with its self-pleasing and self-exaltation and bear the cross in fellowship with Him, and we shall be made partakers of His victory.

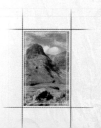

JUNE 10

SELF-DENIAL

"If any man will come after Me, let him deny himself, and take up his cross, and follow Me."
Matthew 16:24

When Jesus Christ came to restore man to his original place, *"He emptied Himself,* taking the form of a servant, and humbled Himself even to the death of the cross." What He has done Himself He asks of all who desire to follow Him. The surrender to Christ is to be so entire, that self is never allowed to come down from the cross to which it has been crucified but is ever kept in the place of death. Let us listen to Jesus, "Deny self," and ask that by the grace of the Holy Spirit we may ever live as those in whom self has been crucified with Christ and in whom the crucified Christ now lives as Lord and Master.

June 11

HE CANNOT BE MY DISCIPLE

*"If any man cometh unto Me, and hateth
not his own life, he cannot be My disciple."*
Luke 14:26

Nothing less than the hating of our own life will make us willing to bear the cross. The soul that seeks to love God cannot but hate the old man which is corrupt through its whole being. Christ claims all. Christ undertakes to satisfy every need and to give a hundredfold more than we give up. It is when by faith we become conscious of what it means to know Christ and to love Him and to receive from Him what can in very deed enrich and satisfy our immortal spirits, that we shall count the surrender of what at first appeared so difficult, our highest privilege.

JUNE 12

FOLLOW ME

*"Go thy way, sell whatsoever thou hast,
come, take up the cross, and follow Me."*
Mark 10:21

Christ reveals from the side of God what is needed to give men the will and the power thus to sacrifice all, if they were to enter the Kingdom. It is only by Divine power that a man can take up his cross, can lose his life, can deny himself and hate the life to which he is by nature so attached. What multitudes have felt that Christ's claims were beyond their reach and have sought to be Christians without any attempt at the whole-hearted devotion and the entire self-denial which Christ asks for! It is only by putting our trust in the living God that we can attempt to be disciples who forsake all and follow Christ.

JUNE 13

A GRAIN OF WHEAT

"Except a grain of wheat fall into the earth and die, it abideth by itself alone; but if it die, it beareth much fruit."
John 12:24 RV

All nature is the parable of how the losing of a life can be the way of securing a truer and a higher life. Every grain of wheat, every seed throughout the world, teaches the lesson that through death lies the path to beautiful and fruitful life. It was so with the Son of God. He had to pass through death in all its bitterness and suffering before He could rise to heaven and impart His life to His redeemed people. Surely the thought that the power of the eternal Life is working in us ought to make us willing and glad to die the death that brings us into the fellowship and the power of life in a risen Christ.

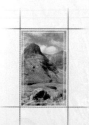

JUNE 14

THY WILL BE DONE

"O My Father, if it be possible, let this cup pass away from Me: nevertheless, not as I will but as Thou wilt."
Matthew 26:39 RV

The highest and the holiest that the Holy Spirit can work in us is to take us up and to keep us in the fellowship of the cross of Christ. It is from Christ alone that we can learn what it means to have fellowship with His sufferings and to be made conformable unto His death.

"Thy will be done"; let this be the deepest and highest word in thy life. In the power of Christ with whom thou hast been crucified and in the power of His Spirit, the daily surrender to the ever-blessed will of God will become the joy and the strength of thy life.

JUNE 15

THE LOVE OF THE CROSS

"Then said Jesus: 'Father, forgive them;
for they know not what they do.'"
Luke 23:34

Christ prays for His enemies. In the hour of their triumph over Him and of the shame and suffering which they delight in showering on Him, He pours out His love in prayer for them. It is the call to everyone who believes in a crucified Christ to go and do likewise. We must not only pray for His enemies, but prove our love to Him and to all who belong to Him, by seeing to it that every one is comforted. Whether it was the love that prayed for His enemies, or the love that cared for His friends, or the love that rejoices over the penitent sinner – in all Christ proves that the Cross is a Cross of love.

JUNE 16

THE SACRIFICE OF THE CROSS

"My God, My God, why hast Thou forsaken Me?"
Matthew 27:46

How deep must have been the darkness that overshadowed Him, when not one ray of light could pierce and He could not say, "My Father"! It was this awful desertion that caused Him the agony and the bloody sweat in Gethsemane. It was His love to God and love to man, yielding Himself to the very uttermost. It is as we learn to believe and to worship that love, that we too shall learn to say: "Abba, Father, Thy will be done."

And then came the great word: "It is finished." All that there was to suffer and endure had been brought a willing sacrifice; He had finished the work the Father gave Him to do. His love held nothing back.

JUNE 17

THE DEATH OF THE CROSS

"'Father, into Thy hands I commit My spirit.'"
Luke 23:46

He gives up His spirit into the power of death, gives up all control over it, to sink down into the darkness and death of the grave where He can neither think, nor pray, nor will. He surrenders Himself to the utmost into the Father's hands, trusting Him to care for Him in the dark and in due time to raise Him up again. Like Him we cast ourselves upon God and depend simply and absolutely upon God to raise us up into the new life. In us there will be fulfilled the wonderful promise concerning the exceeding greatness of His power, according to the mighty power which He wrought in Christ.

JUNE 18

IT IS FINISHED

*"When Jesus had received the vinegar,
He said: 'It is finished.'"*
John 19:30

With that word He uttered the truth of the gospel of our redemption, that all that was needed for man's salvation had been accomplished on the cross. This disposition should characterize every follower of Christ. The mind that was in Him must be in us – *to do the Will of God in all things and to finish His work*. In every case, we may find strength to perform our duty in Christ's word: "It is finished." Faith in what Christ accomplished on the cross will enable you to manifest in daily life the spirit of the cross.

JUNE 19

DEAD TO SIN

"We who died to sin, how shall we any longer live therein?"
Romans 6:2

Our death to sin in Christ delivers us from its power so that we no longer may or need to live in it. The secret of true and full holiness is by faith and in the power of the Holy Spirit to live in the consciousness: I am dead to sin. Quietly ponder these words until the truth masters you. As we grow in the consciousness of our union with the crucified Christ, we shall experience that the power of His life in us has made us free from the power of sin. It is only as the Holy Spirit makes Christ's death a reality within us that we shall know, in the reality of the power of a Divine life, that we are in every deed dead to sin. It only needs the continual living in Christ.

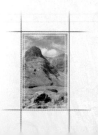

JUNE 20

THE RIGHTEOUSNESS OF GOD

*"Abraham believed God, and it
was counted unto him for righteousness."*

Romans 4:3

There are two essential needs in the redemption of man in Christ Jesus: the need of justification by faith, to restore man to the favor of God. But he must also be quickened to a new life. Just as justification is by faith alone, so is regeneration also. Christ died for our sins; He was raised again out of or through our justification. Paul expounds the wonderful union with Christ through faith by which we died with Him, by which we live in Him, and by which through the Holy Spirit we are made free not only from the punishment but from the power of sin.

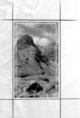

JUNE 21

DEAD WITH CHRIST

*"If we died with Christ, we believe
that we shall also live with Him."*
Romans 6:8

The reason that God's children live so little in the power of the resurrection life of Christ is that they have so little understanding of their death with Christ. It is only as we know that we are dead with Him that we can live with Him. The Word gives us a Divine assurance of what we actually are and have in Christ. This is not a truth that our minds can master and appropriate, but a reality which the Holy Spirit will reveal within us. In His power we accept our death with Christ on the cross as the power of our daily life. If we died with Christ we too have the assurance that in Him we have the power to live unto God.

JUNE 22

DEAD TO THE LAW

"Ye were made dead to the law, through the body of Christ."
Romans 7:4

The believer is not only dead to sin but dead to the law. This is a deeper truth, giving us deliverance from the thought of a life of effort and failure and opening the way to the life in the power of the Holy Spirit. "Thou shalt" is done away with; the power of the Spirit takes its place. In the latter we have the man who knows that he is in Christ Jesus, dead to sin and alive to God, and by the Spirit has been made free and is kept free from the bondage of sin and of death. Oh that we understood that in our flesh there is no good thing and that there is no deliverance but by yielding to the power of the Spirit and so fulfilling the righteousness of the law.

JUNE 23

THE FLESH CONDEMNED ON THE CROSS

"God, sending His own Son in the likeness of sinful flesh, and for sin, condemned sin in the flesh."
Romans 8:3

In my flesh, which I have from Adam, there dwells no good thing that can satisfy the eye of a holy God! And that flesh can never by any process of discipline, or struggling, or prayer, be made better than it is! But the Son of God in the likeness of sinful flesh – in the form of a man – condemned sin on the cross. All the requirements of God's law will be fulfilled in those who walk by the Spirit and in His power live out the life that Christ won for us on the cross and imparted to us in the resurrection.

JUNE 24

JESUS CHRIST AND HIM CRUCIFIED

*"Jesus Christ and Him crucified. And my preaching
was in demonstration of the Spirit and of power."*
1 Corinthians 2:2, 4

Christ the crucified may be the subject of the preaching
and yet there may be such confidence in human learning
and eloquence that there is nothing to be seen of that
likeness of the crucified Jesus which alone gives preaching
its supernatural, its divine power. It was not only in his
preaching but in his whole disposition that Paul sought
to act in harmony with Christ crucified. He had so
identified with the weakness of the cross and its shame,
that he sought to show forth the likeness and the spirit
of the crucified Jesus. The life of every believer must
bear this hallmark.

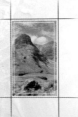

JUNE 25

TEMPERATE IN ALL THINGS

"Every man that striveth in the games
exerciseth self-control in all things ."
1 Corinthians 9:25 RV

Paul here reminds us of the well-known principle that anyone competing in the public game is "temperate in all things". Everything, however attractive, that might be a hindrance in the race is given up in order to obtain an earthly prize. And we who strive for an incorruptible crown and that Christ may be Lord of all – shall we not be temperate in all things that could in the very least prevent our following the Lord Jesus with an undivided heart? We need to pray that this disposition may be found in all Christians through the power of the Holy Spirit.

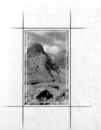

JUNE 26

THE DYING OF THE LORD JESUS

"Bearing about in the body the dying of Jesus, that the life also of Jesus may be manifested in our body."
2 Corinthians 4:10

It is in the crucified Christ and in the fellowship of His death that we are to abide daily and unceasingly. The fellowship of the cross is to be the life of a daily experience. If we are indeed to live for the welfare of others around us, and sacrifice our ease and pleasure to win souls for our Lord, it will be true of us as of Paul, that we are able to say: Death worketh in us, but life in those for whom we pray and labor. It is in the fellowship of the sufferings of Christ that the crucified Lord can live out and work out His life in us and through us.

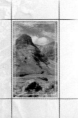

JUNE 27

THE CROSS AND THE SPIRIT

*"How much more shall the blood
of Christ, cleanse your conscience?"*
Hebrews 9:14 RV

Have we not here the reason that our prayers for the mighty working of the Holy Spirit are not more abundantly answered? We have prayed too little that the Holy Spirit might glorify Christ in us in the fellowship and the conformity to His sufferings. The Spirit and the cross are inseparable. The Spirit led Christ to the cross; the cross brought Christ to the throne to receive the fullness of the Spirit to impart to His people. The Holy Spirit can now do nothing more glorious for us than to lead us into the fellowship and the likeness of that crucified life of our Lord.

JUNE 28

THE VEIL OF THE FLESH

*"Having boldness to enter into the holy place
by the blood of Jesus by a new and living way."*
Hebrews 10:19-20

Many Christians can never attain to close fellowship with God because they have never yielded the flesh to the condemnation of the cross. They desire to enter into the holiest of all and yet allow the flesh with its desires and pleasures to rule over them. God grant that we may rightly understand that Christ called us to lose our life that we may live to God with Him. There is no way to a full abiding fellowship with God but through a life with the flesh crucified in Christ Jesus. The Holy Spirit dwells in us to keep the flesh in its place of crucifixion and to give us victory over all temptation.

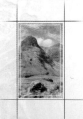

JUNE 29

LOOKING UNTO JESUS

*"Let us run with patience the race that is set before us,
looking unto Jesus, the Author and Perfector of our faith,
who for the joy that was set before Him endured the cross."*
Hebrews 12:1-2 RV

The cross was the way which led to the throne and the
glory of God. It was for the joy set before Him that Christ
endured the cross – the joy of pleasing and glorifying the
Father, of loving and winning souls for Himself. As Christ
found His highest happiness through His endurance of
the cross, so it is only *in our fellowship of the cross* that
we can really become conformed to the image of God's
Son. Awake to this blessed truth and run the race ever
looking to the crucified Jesus. Then you will receive
power to win for Christ the souls He has purchased on
the cross.

JUNE 30

WITHOUT THE GATE

"Jesus also, that He might sanctify the people through His own blood, suffered without the gate."
Hebrews 13:12-13

There are many Christians who love to hear of the boldness with which we can enter into the Holy Place through His blood, who yet are unwilling to separate themselves from the world with the same boldness with which they think to enter the sanctuary. Christians suffer inconceivable loss when they think of entering into the Holy Place in faith and prayer and then feel themselves free to enjoy the friendship of the world so long as they do nothing actually sinful. To be a follower of Christ means to be like Him in His, will to sacrifice self that the Father may be glorified and that others may be saved.

JULY

JULY 1

ALIVE UNTO RIGHTEOUSNESS

"Who His own self bare our sins in His own
body on the tree, that we, having died
unto sins, might live unto righteousness."
1 Peter 2:24 RV

We need the Holy Spirit to make our death to sin in Christ such a reality that we know ourselves to be forever free from its power and so yield our members to God as instruments of righteousness.

We realize by faith how actually we shared with Christ in His death and now, as He lives in us, abide in unceasing fellowship with Him, the Crucified One. This costs self-sacrifice; it costs earnest prayer; it costs a whole-hearted surrender to God and His will and the cross of Jesus; it costs abiding in Christ and unceasing fellowship with Him.

JULY 2

FOLLOWERS OF THE CROSS

*"Hereby know we love, because He laid down His life for us:
and we ought to lay down our lives for the brethren."*
1 John 3:16 RV

Nothing less is expected of us than a Christlike life and a Christlike love proving itself in all our fellowship with believers. It is only as the love of Christ on the cross possesses our hearts and daily animates our whole being, that we shall be able to love one another. It is only as the great truth of the indwelling Christ obtains a place in the faith of the Church, that the Christlike love to one another will become the mark of true Christianity by which the world shall know that we are Christ's disciples. This is what will bring the world to believe that God has loved us even as He loved Christ.

JULY 3

FOLLOWING THE LAMB

*"These are they which follow the
Lamb whithersoever He goeth."*
Revelation 14:4

As the lamb on earth reveals what the Lamb in heaven
would be, so His followers on earth can show forth something of the glory of what it is to follow Him in heaven.
It is the meekness and gentleness and humility that
marked Him which calls for His followers to walk in
His footsteps.

Children of God oh, let Paul's words be the keynote
of your life: "I have been crucified with Christ; yet I live;
and yet no longer I, but Christ liveth in me." Here you
have the way to follow the Lamb even to the glory of the
Throne of God in Heaven.

JULY 4

TO HIM BE THE GLORY

*"Unto Him that loved us, be glory
and dominion forever and ever: Amen."*
Revelation 1:5-6

Love makes everything easy. Do not think of your love to
God but of His great love to you, given through the Holy
Spirit. Meditate on this day and night until you have the
assurance: He loves me unspeakably.

We have here the answer as to what will enable us to
love the fellowship of the crucified Jesus: Nothing less
than His love poured out through the continual inspiration
of the Holy Spirit into the heart of every child of God.
Learn this wonderful song, and repeat it until your heart
is filled with love and joy and courage and turns to Him
in glad surrender day by day: "To Him be the glory and
dominion forever and ever."

JULY 5

THE BLESSING OF THE CROSS

"But God forbid that I should glory, save in the cross of our Lord Jesus Christ"
Galatians 6:14

One of the blessings of the cross consists of this, that it teaches us to know the worthlessness of our efforts and the utter corruption of our own nature. The cross does not offer to improve human nature or to supply what we are unable to do. Many people, indeed, use it in this way, like patching a new cloth on an old garment. But this rends the garment. No, the old garment, our old self, must be laid aside and given over to the death of the cross. The cross brings us to utter bankruptcy of ourselves, and then God can come to our aid.

JULY 6

THE ABIDING PRESENCE

*"I am with you always, even
unto the end of the world."*
Matthew 28:20

The secret of the strength of His disciples would be the
living testimony that Jesus Christ was every moment
with them, inspiring and directing and strengthening
them. In all the work of the minister and the missionary,
everything depends on the consciousness, through a
living faith, of the abiding presence of the Lord with His
servant. If this is clouded, work becomes a human effort
without the freshness and the power of the heavenly life.
And nothing can bring back the power and the blessing
but a return to the Master's feet, for Him to breathe into
the heart in divine power His blessed word: "Lo, I am
with you always!"

July 7

THE OMNIPOTENCE OF CHRIST

"All power is given unto Me in heaven and on earth."
Matthew 28:18

Every disciple of Jesus Christ who desires to take part in the victory that overcometh the world, needs time and faith and the Holy Spirit to come under the full conviction that it is as the servant of the omnipotent Lord Jesus that one is to take part in the work. It is only as Jesus Christ as a living Person dwells and works with His divine energy in our own heart and life that there can be power in our preaching as a personal testimony. It is the disciple of Christ who understands aright that all the power has been entrusted to Christ to be received from Him hour by hour, who will feel the need and experience the power of that precious word: "Lo, I am with you always."

JULY 8

THE OMNIPRESENCE OF CHRIST

"Certainly I will be with thee."
Exodus 3:12

The revelation of God's omnipresence in the man Christ Jesus makes the grace that enables us to claim this presence as our strength and our joy something inexpressibly blessed. And yet how many a servant of Christ, finds it difficult to understand all that is implied in it and how it can become the practical experience of daily life. Everything depends upon faith, accepting Christ's word as a divine reality and trusting the Holy Spirit to make it come true.

Let our faith in Christ, the omnipresent One, be in the quiet confidence that He will every moment keep us in the sure experience of all the light and the strength we need in His service.

July 9

CHRIST: THE SAVIOR OF THE WORLD

"This is indeed the Christ, the Savior of the world."
John 4:42

Omnipotence and Omnipresence are natural attributes of God. They have their true worth only when linked to and inspired by His moral attributes, holiness and love.

It is only when Christ's servants in their lives show that they obey Him in all His commands, that they can expect the fullness of His power and His presence to be with them. The abiding presence of the Savior from sin is promised to all who have accepted Him in the fullness of His redeeming power and who preach by their lives as well as by their words what a wonderful Savior He is.

July 10

Christ Crucified

"God forbid that I should glory, save in the Cross of our Lord Jesus Christ, through which the world hath been crucified unto me, and I unto the world."
Galatians 6:14

It is the crucified Jesus who promises, who offers, to be with me every day. May not this be one reason why we find it so difficult to expect and enjoy the abiding presence? – because we do not glory in the Cross by which we are crucified to the world. How little we have learned, as those who are crucified with Christ, to deny ourselves, to have the mind that was in Christ when He emptied Himself and took the form of a servant and humbled Himself and became obedient even to the death of the Cross.

JULY 11

CHRIST GLORIFIED

*"The Lamb which is in the midst of
the throne shall be their shepherd."*
Revelation 7:17

He who dwelleth in the glory of the Father before whom all heaven bows in prostrate adoration – is none other than He who offers to be my companion, to lead me like a Shepherd. Oh, Christian, do believe that the Lamb in the midst of the throne is in very deed the embodiment of the omnipotent glory of the everlasting God and of His love; and that to have this Lamb of God as your almighty Shepherd and your faithful Keeper does indeed make it possible that the thoughts and the cares of earth shall indeed not prevail to separate you from His love for a single moment.

JULY 12

THE GREAT QUESTION

"Believe ye that I am able to do this?"
Mark 9:28

It is well that we understand clearly what the conditions are on which Christ offers to reveal to us in experience the secret of His abiding presence. God cannot force His blessings on us against our will. He seeks in every possible way to stir our desire and to help us to realize that He is able and most willing to make His promises true. The resurrection of Christ from the dead is His great plea, His all-prevailing argument.

And now the great question comes, whether we are willing to take His word in all simplicity in its divine fullness of meaning and to rest in the promise: "Lo, I am with you all the day."

JULY 13

CHRIST MANIFESTING SELF

*"He that hath My commandments, and
keepeth them, he it is that loveth Me."*
John 14:21

The love with which Christ had loved the disciples had taken possession of their hearts and would show itself in the love of a full and absolute obedience. The Father would see this, and His love would rest upon the soul; Christ would love him with the special love drawn out by the loving heart and would manifest Himself. The love of heaven shed abroad in the heart would be met by the new and blessed revelation of Christ Himself. In the heart thus prepared by the Holy Spirit, showing itself in the obedience of love in a fully surrendered heart, the Father and the Son will take up their abode.

July 14

Mary: The Morning Watch

"Jesus saith unto her; Mary! She turned herself, and saith unto Him, Rabboni! which is to say, Master."
John 20:16

Think of what the morning watch meant to Mary. Is it not a proof of the intense longing of a love that would not rest until it had found the Lord it sought? It meant the struggle of fear against a faith that refused to let go its hold of its wonderful promise. There is nothing that can prove a greater attraction to our Lord than the love that sacrifices everything and rests satisfied with nothing less than Himself. It is to such a love that Christ manifests Himself. He loved us and gave Himself for us. Christ's love needs our love in which to reveal itself. It is love that accepts and rejoices and lives in the word of His promise.

JULY 15

EMMAUS: THE EVENING PRAYER

"They constrained Him saying, Abide with us. And He
went in to tarry with them. And as He sat at meat
with them their eyes were opened, and they knew Him."
Luke 24:29-31

What was it that led our Lord to reveal Himself to these
two men? Nothing less than this, their intense devotion
to their Lord. There may be much ignorance and unbelief,
but if there is a burning desire that above all else longs
for Him, a desire that is ever fostered as the Word is
heard, we may count upon it. To such intense devotion
and constraining prayer, the Lord's message will be given
in power: "Lo, I am with you always"; our eyes will be
opened, and we will know Him and the blessed secret
of the abiding presence always.

JULY 16

THE DISCIPLES: THEIR DIVINE MISSION

"The same day at evening came Jesus and stood in the midst, and saith unto them, Peace be unto you."
John 20:19

The Lord Jesus meets the willing servants whom He had trained for His service and hands over to them the work He had done on earth. He changes their fear into the boldness of peace and gladness. He ascends to the Father; the work the Father had given Him to do He now entrusts to them. He breathes upon them the resurrection power He had won by His death. If our hearts are set on nothing less than the presence of the living Lord, we may count confidently it will be given us.

July 17

Thomas: The Blessedness of Believing

"Blessed are they that have not seen, and yet have believed."
John 20:29

True, living faith gives a sense of Christ's divine nearness far deeper and more intimate than even the joy that filled the heart of Thomas. To those who see not, yet believe, simply, only, truly, fully, believe in what Christ is and can be to them every moment, He has promised that He will manifest Himself and that the Father and He will come and dwell in them. This is the heavenly blessing filling the whole heart and life. Where Jesus Christ is the one object of our desire and our confidence, He will manifest Himself in divine power.

JULY 18

PETER: THE GREATNESS OF LOVE

"Peter was grieved because He said the third time, Lovest thou Me? He said, Lord, Thou knowest that I love Thee."
John 21:17

God is love. Christ is the Son of His love. In heaven and on earth, in the Father and in the Son, and in us and in all our work for Him and our care for souls, the greatest thing is love. To everyone who longs to have Jesus manifest Himself – the essential requisite is love. Peter teaches us that such love is not in our power. But such love came to him through the power of Christ's death and His resurrection life. If Peter the self-confident could be so changed, shall not we believe that Christ will work in us the wondrous change too and manifest Himself to a loving heart in all the fullness of His precious word.

JULY 19

JOHN: LIFE FROM THE DEAD

"When I saw Him, I fell at His feet as one dead. And He laid His right hand upon me, saying, Fear not; I am the Living One; and I was dead, and behold, I am alive forevermore."
Revelation 1:17-18

The lesson is a deep and most needful one. The knowledge of Jesus, fellowship with Him, and the experience of His power is not possible without the sacrifice of all that there is in us of the world and its spirit. Let us accept the lesson – through death to life. In the power of Christ Jesus with whom we have been crucified and whose death now works in us, if we will yield ourselves to it, death to sin, death to the world with all its self-pleasing and self-exaltation is to be the deepest law of our spiritual life.

JULY 20

PAUL: CHRIST REVEALED IN HIM

"It was the good pleasure of God to reveal His Son in me."
Galatians 1:15-16

Paul tells us that it pleased God to reveal His Son in him. If you had asked Paul, if Christ so actually lived in him that he no longer lived, what became of his responsibility? The answer was ready and clear: "I live by the faith of the Son of God, who loved me and gave Himself for me." His life was every moment a life of faith in Him who had loved him and given Himself so completely that He had undertaken at all times to be the life of His willing disciple. This is the sum and substance of all Paul's teaching. The indwelling Christ was the secret of his life of faith, the one power, the one aim of all his life and work, the hope of glory.

JULY 21

WHY COULD WE NOT?

"This kind goeth not out but by prayer and fasting."
Matthew 17:21

To have a strong faith in God needs a life in close touch with Him by persistent prayer. We cannot call up faith at our bidding; it needs close communion with God. It needs not only prayer but fasting too in the larger and deeper meaning of that word. It needs the denial of self, the sacrifice of that pleasing of the flesh and the eye and the pride of life which is the essence of a worldly spirit. To gain the prizes of the heavenly life here on earth needs the sacrifice of all that earth can offer. It needs God to satisfy the human heart and work His mighty miracles in it, it needs the whole man, utterly given up to God, to have the power which can cast out every evil spirit.

JULY 22

THE POWER OF OBEDIENCE

"He that hath sent Me is with Me; He hath not left Me alone;
for I do always the things that are pleasing to Him."
John 8:29

Obedience is the proof and the exercise of the love of God that has been shed abroad in our hearts by the Holy Spirit. It comes from love and leads to love, a deeper and a fuller experience of God's love and indwelling. It assures us that what we ask will be given us. It assures us that we are abiding in the love of Christ. It seals our claim to be called the friends of Christ. For the abiding enjoyment of the Holy Presence, simple, full obedience is necessary. Blessed obedience that enables us to abide in His love. Christ did not speak of an impossibility; He saw what in the power of the Spirit we might confidently expect.

JULY 23

THE POWER OF INTERCESSION

"We will continue steadfastly in prayer."
Acts 6:4

Immeasurably more important than any other work is the linking of all we do to the fountain of Divine life and energy. The Christian world has not only a right to expect mission leaders to set forth the facts and methods of the work, but also a larger discovery of superhuman resources and a greater irradiation of spiritual power. They confess the need of the presence and the power of God's Spirit in their life and work. Shall we not make a part of that great army that pleads with God for that enduement of power which is so necessary for effective work? Shall we not, like the early Apostles, "continue steadfastly in prayer," until God sends an abundant answer?

July 24

The Power of Time

"My times are in Thy hand."
Psalm 31:15

The very essence of religion lies in the thought: Time with God. Time spent alone with God will indeed bring into the lives of His servants the power to enable them to use all their time in His fellowship. Oh, my brothers and sisters who complain that overwork or too much zeal in doing the work is hindering your spiritual efficiency, do you not see that if you would but submit your time-table to the inspection of Christ and His Holy Spirit, you would find that a new life would be yours?

JULY 25

THE POWER OF FAITH

"All things are possible to him that believeth."
Mark 9:23

Faith counts upon God to do all He has promised, as the only measure of its expectation. Faith yields itself to the promise that God will take full possession and all through the day and night inspire hope and expectation. It recognizes the inseparable link that unites God's promises and His commands and yields itself to do the one as fully as it trusts others. This is followed by a faith that begins to see that waiting on God is needed and that quietly rests in the hope of what God will do. This should lead on to an act of decision in which the soul takes God at His word and claims the fulfillment of the promise and then looks to Him to perform what He has spoken.

JULY 26

JOHN'S MISSIONARY MESSAGE

*"And truly our fellowship is with the
Father, and with His Son Jesus Christ."*
1 John 1:3

The message suggests that the very first duty of the
minister or missionary every day is to maintain such
close communion with God that he can preach the truth
in the fullness of joy and with the consciousness that his
life and conversation are the proof that his preaching is
true, so that his words appeal with power to the heart. It
is such teaching, revealing the infinite claim and power
of Christ's love as maintained by the power of the Holy
Spirit, that will encourage and compel us to make the
measure of Christ's surrender for us the only measure
of our surrender to Him and His service.

PAUL'S MISSIONARY MESSAGE

*"God would make known what is the riches
of the glory of this mystery among the Gentiles;
which is Christ in you, the hope of glory."*
Colossians 1:26-27

To Paul's mind, the very center and substance of his Gospel was the indwelling Christ. Though he had been so many years a preacher of this Gospel, he still asked for prayer, that he might make known that mystery aright. Has the church lost the truth of the indwelling Christ? We speak of Paul's missionary methods, but is there not a greater need of Paul's missionary message as it culminates in the one word: "Christ in you, the hope of glory"? Paul felt the need of much prayer to enable him to give the message aright.

JULY 28

THE MISSIONARY'S LIFE

"Ye are witnesses, and God also, how holily
and righteously and unblameably we
behaved ourselves toward you that believe."
1 Thessalonians 2:10 RV

Christ taught His disciples as much by His life as by
His teaching. Paul sought to be a living witness to the
truth of all that he preached about Christ. It is only in
proportion as the missionary can manifest the character
of Christ in and through his own life that he can gain a
hearing for the Gospel.

Believe that when Paul said, "Christ liveth in me, I
live no more," he spoke of an actual, divine, unceasing,
abiding of Christ in him, working in him from hour to
hour all that was well-pleasing to the Father.

JULY 29

THE HOLY SPIRIT

"The Comforter shall glorify Me: for He shall
receive of Mine, and shall show it unto you."
John 16:14

Let no one say: "The experience of Christ's being with us
every day and all day is impossible." Christ came as God
to make known the Father, and the Spirit came as God
to make known the Son in us. We need to understand
that the Spirit as God claims absolute subjection and is
willing to take possession of our whole being and enable
us to fulfill all that Christ asks of us. It is the Spirit who
can deliver us from all the power of the flesh, who can
conquer the power of the world. It is the Spirit through
whom Christ Jesus will manifest Himself to us in nothing
less than His abiding presence.

July 30

Filled With the Spirit

"Be filled with the Spirit."
Ephesians 5:18 RV

If we had the expression, "filled with the Spirit", only in regard to the story of Pentecost, we might naturally think that it was something special and not meant for ordinary life. But our text teaches us the great lesson that it is meant for every Christian and for everyday life. It is only as we are filled with the Spirit that the words of Jesus can be fully understood and experienced: "Lo, I am with you always." If we are to follow Christ, to have His mind in us, to live out His life, we must seek to regard the fullness of the Spirit as a daily provision. It is only as we are led by the Spirit that we can abide in Christ.

JULY 31

THE CHRIST LIFE

"Christ is our life."
Colossians 3:4

Christ's life was more than His teaching, more than His work, more even than His death. It was His life in the sight of God and man that gave value to what He said and did and suffered. And it is this life, glorified in the resurrection, that He imparts to His people and enables them to live out before others. It is the simplicity and intensity of our life in Christ and of the life of Christ Jesus in us, that sustains us in the daily drudgery of work, that makes us conquer self and everything that could hinder the Christ life, and gives the victory over the powers of evil. It is the secret experience of the life hid with Christ in God that enables us to overcome every difficulty.

AUGUST

AUGUST 1

THE CHRISTLIKE LIFE

"Have this mind in you, which was also in Christ Jesus."
Philippians 2:5

And what was the mind that was in Christ Jesus? "Being in the form of God, He emptied Himself, taking the form of a servant, being made in the likeness of men; He humbled Himself, becoming obedient even unto death, yea, the death of the Cross." Self-emptying and self-sacrificing, obedience to God's will, and love to the world, such was the character of Christ for which God so highly exalted Him. Such is the character of Christ that we are to imitate. He was made in the likeness of human flesh, that we might be conformed into the likeness of God. Let us not rest until our faith lays hold of the promise, "It is God that worketh in us."

AUGUST 2

CHRIST: THE NEARNESS OF GOD

"Draw nigh to God, and He will draw nigh to you."
James 4:8

That means, at the beginning of each day afresh to yield ourselves for His holy presence to rest upon us. It means giving time and all our heart and strength to allow Him to reveal Himself. It is impossible to expect the abiding presence of Christ with us through the day, unless there is the definite daily exercise of strong desire and childlike trust. Then the simple offering of ourselves in everything to do His will and seek to please Him. Then comes the quiet assurance of faith, even if there is not much sense of His presence, that God is with us, and that as we go out to do His will, He will watch over us and keep us and strengthen us in the inner man with divine strength for the work we have to do for Him.

AUGUST 3

LOVE

*"Jesus, having loved His own which were
in the world, loved them unto the end."*
John 13:1

Can words make it plainer that God's love to Christ is
given to pass into us and to become our life, that the
love wherewith the Father loved the Son is to be in us?
If we are to claim His daily presence with us, it can only
be as a relationship of infinite tender love between Him
and us, love rooted in the faith of God's love to Christ
coming into our hearts and showing itself in obedience
to His commandments and in love to one another. It is
only in the atmosphere of a holy, living love that the
abiding presence of the loving Christ can be known, and
the depth of the Divine love expressed.

AUGUST 4

THE TRIAL AND TRIUMPH OF FAITH

" Lord, I believe; help Thou mine unbelief."
Mark 9:24

What a lesson! Of all things that are possible to faith, the most impossible is that I should be able to exercise such faith. The abiding presence of Christ is possible to faith. And this faith is possible to the soul that clings to Christ and trusts Him. As surely as He will lead us into His abiding presence all the day, so surely will He strengthen us with divine power for the faith that claims and receives the promise. Blessed the hour when the believer sees how entirely he is dependent on Christ for the faith as well as the blessing and, in the consciousness of the unbelief that is still struggling within, he casts himself upon the power and the love of Jesus.

AUGUST 5

EXCEEDING ABUNDANTLY

"Now unto Him that is able to do exceeding abundantly
above all that we ask or think, according to
the power that worketh in us, unto Him be glory ..."
Ephesians 3:20-21

Paul began his great prayer, "I bow my knees to the Father." He ends it by bringing us to our knees, to give glory to Him as able to fulfill every promise, to reveal Christ dwelling in our hearts and keep us in that life of love which leads to being filled with all the fullness of God. Child of God, bow in deep adoration, giving glory to God, until your heart learns to believe; the prayer will be fulfilled, Jesus Christ will dwell in my heart by faith.

AUGUST 6

THE ONE THING NEEDFUL

"If it be asked, What this one thing is; *It is the Spirit of God brought again to His first power of life in us.* The end and design of all that is written in Scripture is to call us back from the spirit of Satan, the flesh, and the world, to be again under the *full Dependence upon and Obedience to the Spirit of God.*" *

Let us remember the great question is whether we have taken the instruction to heart. Do we indeed believe that this is the one thing needful for the Church and ourselves, the deep conviction that God's one desire is that the Holy Spirit should have the place in us that He had in Adam before the Fall, so that the only thing that gives value to our religion is that it is the immediate work of the Spirit of God?

* William Law, *A Serious Call to a Devout and Holy Life* (1728).

August 7

Total Dependence on God Alone

"All that is called Divine goodness and virtue in the creature is nothing else but the one goodness of God manifesting a discovery of itself in the creature. Goodness, forever and ever, can only belong to God as essential to Him.

"The ground of all true religion, is this; *a total unalterable dependence on God, continual receiving of every degree of goodness and happiness from God alone.* Nothing can be the good of religion, but the power and presence of God *really and essentially living and working in it.* So that the creature must have all its religious goodness as wholly and solely from God's immediate operation, as it had its first goodness at its creation."*

* William Law, *A Serious Call to a Devout and Holy Life (1728).*

AUGUST 8

CONTINUAL INSPIRATION

"All true religion is, or brings forth, an essential union and communion of the spirit of the creature with the Spirit of the Creator.

"No man can reach God with his love or have union with Him by it, *but he who is inspired with that one same Spirit of Love* with which God Himself loved from all eternity. Infinite hosts of new-created heavenly beings can begin no new kind of love to God, nor have the least power of beginning to love Him at all, but so far as *His own Holy Spirit of Love* is brought to life. *Therefore the continual inspiration or operation of the Holy Spirit is the one only possible ground of our continually loving God.*"*

* William Law, *A Serious Call to a Devout and Holy Life* (1728).

AUGUST 9

THE SPIRIT OF GOD IN ADAM

"Divine inspiration was *essential* to man's first created state. The Spirit of the Triune God, breathed into him, was that alone which made him a holy creature in the image and likeness of God. This makes it plain that the work of redemption must be *solely and immediately* the work of the Holy Spirit. And *continual inspiration* is as necessary as man's continuance in his redeemed state. That alone which begins or gives life must be the only continuance or preservation of life. Because without Christ we can do nothing, we ought to believe, expect, wait for, and depend upon His continual immediate operation in everything that we do, through His Spirit dwelling in us."*

* William Law, *A Serious Call to a Devout and Holy Life (1728).*

AUGUST 10

THE MINISTRATION OF THE SPIRIT

"Christ taught His disciples to expect the coming of a higher and more blessed state, which they could not have till *His outward teaching in human language was changed into the inspiration and operation of His Spirit in their souls.*

"Two most fundamental truths are demonstrated: First, that the truth and perfection of the Gospel state could not take place till Christ was glorified and His Kingdom among men made wholly and solely a continual, immediate ministration of the Spirit.

"Secondly, that no man can have any true and real knowledge of the spiritual blessings of Christ's redemption or fitness to preach and bear witness of them to the world, *but solely by that same Divine Spirit ...* "*

* William Law, *A Serious Call to a Devout and Holy Life* (1728).

AUGUST 11

OUR DEATH AND LIFE IN CHRIST

"As the work of the Spirit consists in altering that which is the most radical in the soul, bringing forth a new spiritual death and a new spiritual life, it must be true that no one can know or believe the mysteries of Christ's redeeming power, but only and solely *by an inward finding and feeling the operation of them in that new death and new life, both* of which must be effected in the soul of man, or Christ is not known as its salvation. Our salvation is in the life of Jesus Christ in us."*

We need ever to remember that the great work of the Holy Spirit is to reveal Christ in us. Not to the mind as a matter of knowledge, but in the heart and life, communicating to us the very death and life of our Lord. It is thus that Christ is formed in us.

* William Law, *A Serious Call to a Devout and Holy Life* (1728).

249

AUGUST 12

HUMILITY

"Man's intellectual faculties are, by the Fall, in a much worse state than his natural animal appetites, and want a much greater self-denial. We need to know that our salvation consists wholly in being saved *from that which we are by nature.* In the whole nature of things nothing could be salvation or Savior to us, but such *a humility of God* manifested in human nature as is beyond all expression. Self is the whole evil of fallen nature; self-denial is our capacity of being saved, humility is our Savior."*

In the life of faith, humility has a far deeper place than we think. It is not only one among other virtues, but is the first and chief need of the soul.

* William Law, *A Serious Call to a Devout and Holy Life* (1728).

AUGUST 13

THE KINGDOM OF HEAVEN

"'Thy Kingdom come, Thy will be done on earth as it is in heaven.' What is God's Kingdom in heaven but the *manifestation of what God is* and what He does in His heavenly creatures? We daily read this prayer, reminding us that nothing but a continual, essential, immediate, Divine illumination can do that which we pray may be done. How can His will only be done, but where the Spirit that wills in God, wills in the creature?"*

How much has been written about what the Kingdom of heaven means, but here we have what it really is. As God rules in His Kingdom in heaven, so when the kingdom comes into our hearts He lives and rules there. The Kingdom of God consists of those in whom God rules as He does in heaven.

* William Law, *A Serious Call to a Devout and Holy Life (1728)*.

AUGUST 14

THE NATURE OF LOVE

"The Spirit of Love is and must be a will to all goodness, and you do not have the Spirit of Love till you have this will to all goodness at all times and on all occasions. The Spirit of love is not in you till it is the Spirit of your life, till you live freely, willingly and universally according to it.

"The Spirit of Love, wherever it is, is its own blessing and happiness, because it is the truth and the reality of God in the soul. For as love has no by-ends, wills nothing but its own increase, so everything is as oil to its flame. The Spirit of Love does not want to be rewarded or honored; its only desire is to propagate itself and become the blessing and happiness of everything that wants it."*

* William Law, *A Serious Call to a Devout and Holy Life* (1728).

AUGUST 15

THE NECESSITY OF LOVE

"There is no peace, nor ever can be, for the soul of man but in the purity and perfection of its first created nature; nor can it have its purity and perfection in any other way than in and by the Spirit of Love. For as Love is the God that created all things, so Love is the purity, the perfection, and blessing of all created things; and nothing can live in God but as it lives in Love."*

Let us take time to ponder this blessed truth and promise: the God and Father of all love is longing to fill the heart of His children with nothing less than His own Divine, Eternal Love!

* William Law, *A Serious Call to a Devout and Holy Life* (1728).

August 16

Love: A New Birth from Above

"Hold it for a certain truth that you can have no good come into your soul, but only by the one way of a birth from above, from the *Entrance of the Deity* into the properties of your own soulish life. Love is Delight, and Delight cannot arise in any creature until its nature is in a delightful state or is possessed of that in which it must rejoice. Goodness is only a sound and virtue a mere strife of natural passions, till the Spirit of Love is the breath of everything that lives and moves in the heart. For Love is the one only blessing and goodness and God of nature; and you have no true religion or no worship of the one true God but in and by that Spirit of Love which is *God Himself living and working in you*."*

* William Law, *A Serious Call to a Devout and Holy Life* (1728).

AUGUST 17

THE TWO-FOLD LIFE

"No intelligent creature, whether angel or man, can be good and happy, but by partaking of and having in himself a two-fold life. The two-fold life is this: it must have the life of nature and the life of God in it. God Himself cannot make a creature to be in its self or as to its own nature anything else but a state of emptiness, of want, of appetite. The reason is this: it is because *goodness and happiness are absolutely inseparable from God* and can be nowhere but in God. All the dispensations of God whether by the law or the prophets, by the Scriptures or ordinances of the Church are only helps to holiness which they cannot give but are meant to turn the creaturely life from itself and its own working to a faith and hope, a hunger and thirst after that first union with the life of the Deity."*

* William Law, *A Serious Call to a Devout and Holy Life (1728).*

AUGUST 18

PERPETUAL INSPIRATION

"Perpetual inspiration is as necessary to a life of Goodness, Holiness, and Happiness, as the perpetual respiration of the air is necessary to animal life. What a mistake it is to confine inspiration to particular times and occasions, to prophets and apostles when the common Christian looks and trusts *to be continually led and inspired by the Spirit of God.* The holiness of the common Christian is not an occasional thing, but is the holiness of that which is always alive and stirring in us, namely, our thoughts, wills, desires, and affections. If our thoughts and affections are to be always holy and good, then the Holy and Good Spirit of God is to be always operating as a principle of life within us."

* William Law, *A Serious Call to a Devout and Holy Life (1728).*

AUGUST 19

TWO KINDS OF KNOWLEDGE

"Every kind of virtue and goodness may be brought into us by two different ways. They may be taught us outwardly by men, by rules and precepts; and they may be inwardly born in us as the genuine birth of our own renewed spirit. In the former way, they at best only change our outward behavior, putting our passions under a false restraint.

"If you learn virtue and goodness only from outward means, you will be virtuous or good according to time and place and outward forms. But the Spirit of Prayer, the Spirit of Love, the Spirit of Humility are only to be obtained by the operation of *the Light and Spirit of God,* not outwardly teaching but *inwardly bringing forth a new-born spirit within us.*"*

* William Law, *A Serious Call to a Devout and Holy Life* (1728).

AUGUST 20

THE MONSTER OF SELF

"To die to self or to come from under its power cannot be done by any act of resistance we can make to it by the powers of nature. The only one way of dying to self meets you in everything and is never without success. If you ask what is this one true simple, plain, immediate, and unerring way, *it is the way of Patience, Meekness, Humility, and Resignation to God.*"*

There is not a more difficult lesson in the Christian life than to attain a true knowledge of what self is. Its terrible power, its secret and universal rule, and the blinding influence it exerts in keeping us from the knowledge of what it is are the cause of all our sin and evil. Hence it comes that so few really believe in their absolute inability to obey God or to believe in His love.

* William Law, *A Serious Call to a Devout and Holy Life* (1728).

AUGUST 21

DYING TO SELF

"The reason many are vainly endeavoring after these virtues is because you see them in a multitude of human rules and methods and not in that simplicity of faith in which those who applied to Christ immediately attained that which they asked of Him, 'Come unto Me, all ye that labor and are heavy laden, and I will give you rest.' How short and simple and certain a way to peace and comfort."*

We too often think of faith in Christ only as connected with the work He did for us on the Cross. But its meaning is far larger and richer. It is by faith that we can claim all the grace and the mind there were in Him and receive it through the Spirit as ours.

* William Law, *A Serious Call to a Devout and Holy Life (1728).*

AUGUST 22

OF FAITH IN CHRIST

"In the words of Christ, 'Learn of Me, for I am meek and lowly of heart, and ye shall find rest unto your souls,' you have two truths asserted. First that to be given up to Patience, Meekness, Humility, and Resignation to God is strictly the same thing as to learn of Christ or to have faith in Him. And that because the inclination of your heart toward these virtues is truly giving up all that you are and all that you have from fallen Adam, it is perfectly leaving all that you have and your highest act of faith in Him. The Spirit of Divine Love can have no place or possibility of birth in any fallen creature till it wills and chooses to be dead to all self in a patient, meek, humble, resignation to the good power and mercy of God. Give up yourself to be helped by the mercy of God."*

* William Law, *A Serious Call to a Devout and Holy Life (1728)*.

AUGUST 23

THE LAMB OF GOD

"The sight of the Sabbath of the soul, freed from the miserable labor of self to rest in Meekness, Humility, Patience under the Spirit of God is like the joyful voice of the Bridegroom to my soul and leaves no wish in me but to be at the marriage-feast of the Lamb. This marriage-feast signifies the entrance into the highest state of union that can be between God and the soul in this life. In other words, it is the birthday of the Spirit of Love in our souls which, whenever we attain it, will feast our souls with such peace and joy in God as will blot out the remembrance of everything that we called joy or peace before. As the Lamb of God He has all power to bring forth in us a weariness of our fallen state and a willingness to fall from it into His Meekness and Humility."*

* William Law, *A Serious Call to a Devout and Holy Life (1728).*

AUGUST 24

PRAYER: THE KEY TO THE TREASURES OF HEAVEN

"Man has been sent into the world on no other errand but by prayer to rise out of the vanity of time into the riches of eternity. We have all of us free access to all that is great and good and happy and carry within ourselves *a key to all the treasures that Heaven has to bestow upon us.* God is not an absent or distant God, but is more present in and to our souls than our bodies. And we are strangers to heaven and without God in the world for this reason only because we are void of that Spirit of Prayer, which alone can, and never fails to unite us with the one and only good and to open heaven and the Kingdom of God within us."*

* William Law, *A Serious Call to a Devout and Holy Life* (1728).

AUGUST 25

THE GOODNESS OF GOD

"This is the amiable nature of God; He is the Good, the unchangeable overflowing fountain of good, that sends forth nothing but good to all eternity. Oh, how sweet is this contemplation of the height and depth of the riches of the Divine Love! With what attractions must it draw every thoughtful person to return Love for Love to this overflowing fountain of boundless goodness!"*

With what joy an invalid on a winter's day yields himself to bask in the bright sunshine. What journeys are undertaken to the heights in Switzerland where the sun gives its warmth best. And, alas! how little God's children understand that this is just the one thing they need, to wait before God in quiet till His light shines upon them and into them and through them.

* William Law, *A Serious Call to a Devout and Holy Life (1728)*.

AUGUST 26

THE KINGDOM OF SELF

"Man by his fall had fallen from a life in God *into a life of self*, an animal life of self-love, self-esteem, and self-seeking in the poor perishing enjoyments of the world. You know now to what it is that you are daily to die and daily to live; and therefore look upon every day as lost that does not help forward both this death and this life in you. Casting yourself with a broken heart at the feet of the Divine Mercy, desire nothing but that every moment of your life may be given to God, and pray from the bottom of your heart that the seed of eternity, the spark of life that had so long been smothered under earthly rubbish, might breathe and come to life in you."*

* William Law, *A Serious Call to a Devout and Holy Life (1728).*

AUGUST 27

CONTINUAL SELF-DENIAL

"To think of anything in religion or to pretend to real holiness *without totally dying to this old man* is building castles in the air. To think of being alive in God before we are dead to our own nature is as impossible as for a grain of wheat to be alive before it dies. The total dying to self is the only foundation of a solid piety."*

Our blessed Lord Jesus could not be raised from the dead into the glory of the Father's right hand until He had died on the Cross. This is the new and living way which He opened up through the rent veil of the flesh into the Holiest of All. And it is in this new and living way with our flesh also crucified and given over to death, that we can enter into the life and the joy of God's presence here upon earth.

* William Law, *A Serious Call to a Devout and Holy Life (1728).*

August 28

Prayer: A State of the Heart

"As a spirit of longing after the life of this world made Adam and us to be poor pilgrims on earth, so the Spirit of prayer or *the longing desire of the heart after Christ and God and heaven* and raises us out of the miseries of time into the riches of eternity."*

First there is the continual streaming forth of the infinite love of God toward us. Then the continual dependence upon God every hour. Then the continual receiving of goodness and happiness from God alone. Then the continual mortification of our evil nature; then the continual and immediate inspiration of the Holy Spirit. Then the continual breathing of the heart after God in prayer, and then the continual loving of Him with our whole heart.

* William Law, *A Serious Call to a Devout and Holy Life (1728).*

AUGUST 29

A WORLDLY SPIRIT

"Choose any life but the life of God and heaven, and you choose death, for death is nothing else but the loss of the life of God. *A worldly, earthly spirit can know nothing of God.* All real knowledge is Life or a living sensibility of the thing that is known as far as our life reaches, so far we understand and know, and no further. All after this is only the play of our imagination amusing itself with the dead pictures of its own ideas."*

When our Lord spoke of the world, its prince, and its spirit, He ever laid stress on its hatred of Him and His Church. And so His Apostles, too, warned most earnestly against being conformed to the world. "If a man love the world, the love of the Father is not in him."

* William Law, *A Serious Call to a Devout and Holy Life (1728).*

AUGUST 30

OF THE DESPAIR OF SELF

"There is no true and real conversion from the life of sin and death till a man comes to know that nothing less than his whole nature is to be parted with and yet finds in himself no possibility of doing it. Till all is despair in ourselves, faith and hope and turning to God in prayer are only things practiced by rule and method; they are not living qualities of a new birth till we have done feeling any trust or confidence in ourselves."*

Let us seek above everything to believe that God is love and as such longs intensely to fill every heart with its blessedness. As the sun shines upon the earth with the one great object of shedding on it its light and its life, do let us believe that the great God of love is shining upon us every moment of the day.

* William Law, *A Serious Call to a Devout and Holy Life* (1728).

AUGUST 31

TRUE RELIGION

"Here you should once for all mark where and what the true nature of religion is; its work and effect is *within;* its glory, its life, its perfection is all within. It is merely and solely the raising a new life, new love, and a new birth in the inward spirit of our heart. It is nothing else *but the power and life and Spirit of God,* as Father, Son, and Holy Spirit working, creating, and reviving life in the fallen soul and driving all its evil out of it."*

Oh, let us seek to study what God counts true religion. Nothing less than this, that He Himself, by His Spirit, should live and work in us as the Light and the Life of our souls. It is this which will enable us continually to worship, to pray, and to work in His holy Presence.

* William Law, *A Serious Call to a Devout and Holy Life (1728).*

SEPTEMBER

SEPTEMBER 1

THE PRACTICE OF PRAYER

"The only infallible way to go safely through all the difficulties, trials, dryness, or opposition of our evil tempers is *to expect nothing from ourselves* but in everything expect and depend upon God for relief. Prayer can only be taught you by awakening in you a true sense and knowledge of what you are and what you should be, and filling you with a continual longing desire of the heart after God, His life, and Holy Spirit."*

How strange that our highest privilege, holding fellowship with God in prayer, is to so many a burden and a failure and to so many more a matter of form without the power. Let us learn the lesson that to expect nothing from ourselves is the first step and then truly with the heart to expect everything from God.

* William Law, *A Serious Call to a Devout and Holy Life (1728).*

SEPTEMBER 2

A TOUCHSTONE OF TRUTH

"Offer this one prayer to God: 'That of His great goodness, He would make known to you and take from your heart every kind and form and degree of pride, whether it be from evil spirits or your own corrupt nature and that He would awaken in you the deepest depths and truth of that humility which can make you capable of His light and His Holy Spirit.'"*

Prayer is the highest revelation of our fitness for fellowship with God. It begins with the deep humility that knows that it is nothing, that has no desire but to meet God in the fellowship of His love and then with the whole being continually to live in absolute surrender to Him.

* William Law, *A Serious Call to a Devout and Holy Life* (1728).

SEPTEMBER 3

THE SPIRIT OF PRAYER

"The spirit of the soul is in itself nothing else but a spirit breathed forth from the life of God and for this only end, that the life of God, the nature of God, the working of God, the tempers of God might be manifested in it. The Spirit of Prayer is a pressing forth of the soul out of this earthly life; it is a stretching with all its desires after the life of God; it is a leaving, as far as it can, all its own spirit to receive a Spirit from above, to be one Life, one Love, one Spirit with Christ in God. This prayer, which is an emptying itself of all its own natural tempers and an opening itself for the Light and Love of God to enter into it, is the prayer in the name of Christ to which nothing is denied."*

* William Law, *A Serious Call to a Devout and Holy Life (1728).*

September 4

The Prayer of the Heart

"Turning to God according to the inward feeling, want, and motion of your own heart in love, in trust, in faith of having from Him all that you want and wish to have – this turning unto God, whether it be with or without words, is the best form of prayer in the world. For prayers not formed according to the real state of your heart are but like a prayer to be pulled out of a deep well when you are not in it. When the heart really pants and longs after God, its prayer is a praying moved and animated by the Spirit of God; it is *the breath or inspiration of God, stirring, moving, and opening itself in the heart.*"*

Our times of prayer are meant to lead us on to a life of prayer in which the heart will continually live and rejoice in God's presence.

* William Law, *A Serious Call to a Devout and Holy Life* (1728).

SEPTEMBER 5

THE PROOF OF THE SPIRIT

"The Holy Spirit of God is as necessary to our Divine life as the air of this world is necessary to our animal life and is as distinct from and as much without us as the air of this world is distinct from the creatures that live in it. And yet our own good spirit is the very Spirit of God moving and stirring in us, and yet not God, but the Spirit of God breathed into a creaturely form; and this good Spirit, Divine in its origin, and Divine in its nature, is that alone in us that can reach God, unite with Him, be moved and blessed by Him. If it is the earnest desire and longing of your heart to be merciful as He is merciful, to be full of His unwearied Patience, to dwell in His unalterable Meekness; if you long to be like Him in impartial Love, you have *the utmost certainty that the Spirit of God lives, dwells, and governs in you.*"*

* William Law, *A Serious Call to a Devout and Holy Life (1728).*

SEPTEMBER 6

LOVE AND FAITH

"This is His commandment, that we should believe in the name of His Son Jesus Christ, and love one another."
1 John 3:23

The Church must learn not only to preach the love of God in redemption; it must go further and teach Christians to show that the love of Christ is in their hearts by love shown to the brethren. Our Lord called this a new commandment – a badge by which the world should recognize His disciples! There is great need for this preaching of love. A life of great holiness will result if we really love each other as Christ loves us. May we understand the two manifestations of love: God's wonderful love in Christ to us and the wonderful love in us, through the Holy Spirit, to God and our brethren.

SEPTEMBER 7

FAITH AND LOVE

*"Your faith groweth exceedingly, and the love of
each of you all toward one another aboundeth."*
2 Thessalonians 1:3

These expressions of the Apostle Paul show us the true
connection between faith and love in the life of the Christian. Faith always comes first; it roots itself deeply in the
love of God and bears fruit in love to the brethren. As
in nature the root and the fruit are inseparable, so is it
with faith and love in the realm of grace. As we cultivate
faith in God's love, our hearts will be *filled with love to
the brethren.* The genuineness of our faith in the love of
God must be shown by love in our daily lives.

SEPTEMBER 8

THE LOVE OF GOD

*"God is love, and he that dwelleth in
love dwelleth in God, and God in him."*
1 John 4:16

The glory of God in heaven is that He has a Will to all
that is good. That includes the two meanings of the word:
good, all that is right and perfect: *good,* all that makes
happy. The God who wills nothing but good is a God of
love. The characteristic of Love is that she "seeketh not
her own." *This self-same love of God, Christ has poured
into our hearts through the Holy Spirit* so that our whole
life may be permeated with its vital power. This love is
the possession of all who are of Christ and streams forth
from them to take the whole world within its compass.

SEPTEMBER 9

THE LOVE OF CHRIST

"The love of Christ constraineth us."
2 Corinthians 5:14

God's desire is that on this sinful earth His love should take possession of our hearts. With this purpose He gave on the cross the greatest proof of love the world has ever seen. He took our sins upon Him, that friend and foe alike might know God's eternal love. After the Lord Jesus had ascended to heaven, *He gave the Holy Spirit to shed abroad this love in our hearts.* The disciples, impelled by the love of Christ, in turn offered their lives to make it known to others.

O Christians, think this over: God longs to have our hearts wholly filled with His love. Then He will be able to use us as channels for this love to flow out to others.

SEPTEMBER 10

THE LOVE OF THE SPIRIT

"The love of God hath been shed abroad in our hearts through the Holy Spirit, which was given unto us."
Romans 5:5

O Christian, believe that the love of God will work in your heart as a vital power to enable you to love God and to love the brethren. Cease to expect the least love in yourself. Believe in the power of God's love resting on you and abiding in you, teaching you to love God and the brethren, with His own love. The Spirit will enable us to love God and other Christians and even our enemies. Be assured of two things. First, that in your own strength you cannot love God or other Christians. And, second, that the Holy Spirit is within you every day and every hour, to fill you with the Spirit of love.

SEPTEMBER 11

THE POWER OF LOVE

"We are more that conquerors through Him that loved us."
Romans 8:37

In days of unrest and strong racial feeling, we need above all a new discovery and living experience of the love of God. God's power by which He rules and guides the world is the power of an undying, persistent love. He works through the hearts and spirits and wills of men and women, wholly yielded to Him and His service; and He waits for them to open their hearts to Him in love and then, full of courage, to become witnesses for Him. Our faith in Love, as the greatest power in the world, should prepare us for a life in communion with God in prayer and for a life of unselfish service among those around us.

SEPTEMBER 12

THE SIGN OF A TRUE CHURCH

"By this shall all men know that ye are My
disciples, if ye have love one to another."
John 13:35

In God, love reaches its highest point and is the culmination of His glory. Love is the power that moved Christ to die for us. In love, God highly exalted Him as Lord and Christ. Love is the power that broke our hearts, and love is the power that healed them. Love is the power through which Christ dwells in us and works in us. Love can change my whole nature and enable me to surrender all to God. It gives me strength to live a holy, joyous life, full of blessing to others. Every Christian should show forth the love of God. We may and can love with *God's own love,* which is poured forth unto our hearts by the Holy Spirit.

SEPTEMBER 13

RACE-HATRED

*"For we also were sometimes foolish, living in malice
and envy, hateful, and hating one another."*
Titus 3:3

What a dark picture of the state of human nature and of
human society! No wonder that man's love of his own
people, implanted in his heart by nature, soon changed
to hatred of other peoples. Love of country became the
fruitful source of race-hatred, war, and bloodshed. God
has placed races side by side to see if our Christianity
will enable us to overcome race-hatred and in the power
of Christ's love prove that "in the new creature ... all
are one in Christ Jesus." What an opening there is for
the Church of Christ and her ministers to preach and
proclaim the love of God.

SEPTEMBER 14

"LOVE YOUR ENEMIES"

"Thou shalt love thy neighbor and hate thine enemy."
Matthew 5:43

It was the Jewish Rabbis in Christ's earthly day who said this. How often the Christian follows the example of the Jewish teachers! The command of our Lord is too strict and narrow for us; we have not yielded ourselves to God in obedience to the new commandment to love other Christians with Christ's love, believing that this love will flow out to all around, even to those who hate us. This will require much grace and will cost time and trouble and much earnest prayer. Day by day we learn that there is only one way to love our enemies: by the love of Christ sought and found in prayer.

September 15

Forgive, but Not Forget

"I will forgive their iniquity, and I will remember their sin no more."
Jeremiah 31:34

"Forgive – yes, but forget – never." Many have allowed themselves to be deceived by these words. I have often seen a dog come in at the front door to seek coolness and shade. He would be driven out, and the door closed but would go in again through the back door. The front door is: "I will forgive." One wishes to put away all thought of hatred or ill-feeling. But see how quickly and quietly these evil thoughts come back through the back door of "I will never forget." Many a one trusts in God's forgiving love, but does not remember that when God forgives, He forgets.

SEPTEMBER 16

AS GOD FORGIVES

*"Forgive us our sins; for we forgive
every one that is indebted to us."*
Luke 11:4

The forgiveness of sins is the great all-embracing gift by
which, in His mercy, God sets the sinner free and receives
him back into His love and favor. It gives us boldness
toward God and is the source of our salvation; it gives us
cause for thankfulness every day. It is God's will and our
souls feel the need of it, that we should each day walk
with Him, as those whose sins are forgiven and who are
living in the light of His countenance. As we walk with
God in the full assurance of sins forgiven, He desires that
in our fellowship with those around us, too, we should
live as those who have been freely forgiven.

SEPTEMBER 17

THE PREACHING OF LOVE

"The greatest of these is Love."
1 Corinthians 13:13

If there was a revival of the preaching of love, more than one minister would have to say: "There is such a lack of love in my own heart; how can I teach others?"

Often in preaching or in writing, I have asked myself: But do you possess what you preach to others? And I have followed the advice: *Preach it because you believe it to be the teaching of God's Word, and heartily desire it.* Preach the truth by faith, and the experience will follow. Let the minister who feels impelled to preach about love not hesitate to do so, and he will soon be able to preach it because he has himself received that which he commends.

SEPTEMBER 18

THE LEADERS

*"I exhort, therefore, that first of all supplications,
prayers, intercessions, thanksgivings, be made for
all men; for kings and all that are in authority."*
1 Timothy 2:1-2

Would it not be sad if we came into God's presence
divided into camps, praying one against the other? We
must pray for our leaders and for *all* who are in authority.
As leaders of the people, their influence for good or evil
is inexpressible. Their hearts are in God's hands, and He
can turn them whithersoever He wills. Let our prayers
ascend to God in all sincerity, and He will hear and grant
that which is good for the whole land.

SEPTEMBER 19

UNFEIGNED LOVE
OF THE BRETHREN

"Seeing ye have purified your souls through the
Spirit, love one another with a pure heart."
1 Peter 1:22

In the days of the Early Church it was clearly understood at conversion that, in confessing Christ, the new convert also promised unfeigned love to the brethren.

God's Word is a mirror into which the Church and each individual member must look, to see that we are truly Christian, showing by our conduct that we take God's Word as our rule of life. If our hearts condemn us, we must turn at once to God, confessing our sin. Let us believe that *the Spirit of love does indeed dwell in us.*

SEPTEMBER 20

THE SPIRIT OF LOVE

"God hath given us the spirit of love."
2 Timothy 1:7

This divine love in the heart of the believer is *a little sanctuary, whence the child of God receives power,* in obedience to the inner law of love, to live always in the love of God. This holy love includes Fellowship with God, Union with Christ, and Love to all Christians. How can we attain to this experience? Through *faith alone.* When our eyes have been opened and we realize that the love of God has already been shed abroad in our hearts by His Spirit, enabling us to keep His commandments and to love the brethren – then let us bow in stillness of soul before God and adore the love which has taken possession of our hearts.

SEPTEMBER 21

A SONG OF LOVE

"But now abideth faith, hope, love, these
three; but the greatest of these is love."
1 Corinthians 13:13

Love is the greatest thing in the world. We should read this chapter more often than we do, and commit the Song to memory so that the great words are imprinted on our hearts. Consider all that means. "The greatest of these is love." Let this love rule in your life. O Christian, are you living in a world that is uncharitable and selfish or full of bitterness and hatred? Take refuge under the wings of this everlasting love. Let your heart be filled with it so that by God's almighty power you may be a witness to the transforming power of love. Thus you will be a fountain of blessing to all around you.

SEPTEMBER 22

THE OBEDIENCE OF LOVE

"If ye love Me, ye will keep My commandments."
John 14:15

This precept loses its power because Christians say: "It is quite impossible; I cannot always keep His commandments." Yet our Lord really meant it, for in the last night with His disciples, He promised them definitely a new life in which the power of the Spirit would enable them to live a life of obedience. The Holy Spirit is the power that works within us, both to will and to do, and so prevents the flesh from gaining the upper hand. Believe that the Holy Spirit will cause the love of Christ to work in your heart in such power that you will be able to abide in the love of Jesus the whole day, and to keep His words with great joy.

SEPTEMBER 23

LOVE AND PRAYER

"Be sober, and watch unto prayer, above all
things being fervent in your love among yourselves."
1 Peter 4:7-8

Where the heart is filled with fervent love to others, prayer will continually rise to God for those whom we love and even for those with whom we do not agree. We must never neglect to indicate what an important place prayer holds in the life of love. These two fruits of the Spirit are inseparably connected. If you wish your love to grow and increase, forget yourself and pray, pray earnestly for God's children and His Church. And if you would increase in prayerfulness, give yourself in fervent love to those around you. Love impels to prayer; to believing prayer is granted the love of God.

SEPTEMBER 24

THE FIRST AND GREAT COMMANDMENT

*"Love the LORD the God with all
thy heart and with all thy soul."*
Deuternomy 30:6

God greatly desires our love. It is the nature of all love to long to be acceptable and to meet with response. God longs with a never-ending, fervent desire to have our love, the love of the whole heart. When we take time to wait upon God and remember with what a burning desire God sought to win our love through the gift of His Son, we shall be able to realize that God has a strong and never-ceasing longing for the love of our heart. God will work within me by His Spirit, granting the desire to love Him.

SEPTEMBER 25

THE ROYAL LAW OF LOVE

"If ye fulfill the royal law according to the scripture,
Thou shalt love thy neighbor as thyself, ye do well."
James 2:8

In heaven where God is and on earth among all people, love is the royal law, love is supreme. The Christian's love for others reveals to us our own nature implanted by God, that we should love ourselves, and it calls us to love our neighbors with the same love. Christianity teaches us to love our neighbors because God loves them. Everyone, howsoever vile, has a share in God's compassion and love because each one is made in God's image. I ought, therefore, to love my neighbors, not merely because they are people, but because I see God's likeness in them and because God loves them.

SEPTEMBER 26

NATIONAL FEELING

"God hath made of one blood all nations of men."
Acts 17:26

"Nationality may be regarded as a gift of God, the divine right of each nation according to its special nature to preserve and develop its individuality in the service of the common life of all the world." Without that sanctifying process, national feeling may become the prey of ambition and the source of hatred, aversion and contempt for other nations. It is the holy calling of every Christian to point out the way by which national feeling may attain its twofold aim: (1) the development and uplifting of the people themselves, and (2) the right attitude to other peoples in the upbuilding of all mankind.

ONE STREAM OR TWO STREAMS?

*"The stick of Ephraim, and the stick of Judah, I will make
them one stick, and they shall be one in Mine hand."*
Ezekiel 37:19

One who is really desirous of knowing and doing God's
will must try to understand the two-fold calling: to be
faithful in preserving one's own nationality; and at the
same time to show one's love and appreciation of other
nations with whom, under God's providence, one's lot
has been cast. When Ephraim and Judah became one
in God's hand, the difference between the two was not
destroyed. Each kept separate characteristics but also the
oneness was that of true unity and mutual love. God will
fulfill this promise to us but on one condition: We must
place our people in God's hand by our prayers.

SEPTEMBER 28

PRAY FOR LOVE

*"The Lord make you to increase and abound in
love one toward another, and toward all men."*
1 Thessalonians 3:12

What a prayer! Without love this was impossible. Do
you pray for holiness? Then show it by a hearty love to
all believers. God is love – everlasting endless love. That
love can only be experienced when Christians are knit
together in love and live for others.

O Christian, if you feel as if you cannot pray, take
these words of divine love and ponder them in your
heart. You will gain a strong and a joyous assurance
of what God is able to do for you. He will make you to
abound in love and strengthen your heart to live before
Him in holiness.

SEPTEMBER 29

LIKE CHRIST

"I have given you an example, that ye
should do as I have done to you."
John 13:15

The love of Christ manifested in His death on the cross
is the ground, not only of our hope of salvation, but it is
the only rule for our daily life and conduct. The love of
Christ is my only hope of salvation. A walk in that love
is the way truly and fully to enjoy that salvation.

Faith in Christ's wonderful love and in God's inconceivable love resting upon us, makes it not only possible
but certain that those who keep close to Christ will walk
in love. What a blessed walk in His fellowship, when we
are led by the Holy Spirit and strengthened for a life in
His likeness!

SEPTEMBER 30

THE POWER OF GOD'S WORD

*"The words that I have spoken
unto you are spirit and are life."*
John 6:63

Without faith, great faith, persevering faith, there can be
no thought of the power of love within us. This true faith
is deeper and higher than what we usually mean when
we say we believe God's Word. It bows before God in the
deep realization of His greatness, of His power to work
wonders in our hearts and of His loving care of us.

It is necessary to be deeply convinced of our utter
inability to produce this love which is holy and can
conquer sin and unbelief. We need *a burning desire to
receive this heavenly love into our hearts* whatever the
cost may be.

OCTOBER

OCTOBER 1

PERFECT LOVE
ACCORDING TO 1 JOHN

"He that loveth his brother abideth in the light."
1 John 2:10

"Beloved, if God so loved us, *we ought also to love one another. If we love one another, God dwelleth in us, and his love is perfected in us*" (1 Jn. 4:11-12).

Each of these words is a living seed and has within it a Divine power which is able to take root and grow and bear fruit in our hearts. But just as the seed requires the soil in which it grows to be kept free of all weeds, so the heart must be wholly surrendered to God and His service, that the seed of the Word may bear this heavenly fruit. And love to God and love to one another are inseparable.

OCTOBER 2

THE LOVE THAT SUFFERS

*"Walk in love, as Christ also hath
loved us, and hath given Himself for us."*
Ephesians 5:2

It it not strange that love, which is the source of the greatest happiness, should also be the cause of intense suffering? Our life on earth is such that suffering always follows when love seeks to save the object of its love. It is only by means of suffering that love can gain its end. Even the almighty power of God's love could not achieve its purpose without suffering.

Do you really long to know the love of Christ in all its fullness? Then yield yourself wholly to Him and His blessed service. Let it be your chief delight to live and to suffer for others in the love and fellowship of the Lord Jesus.

OCTOBER 3

THE WORKS OF THE FLESH

"The works of the flesh are manifest; witchcraft, hatred,
strife, jealousies, wrath, envyings, murders ..."
Galatians 5:19-21

It is quite impossible for Christians by their own efforts to lead a life of love. The grace of God will enable the Christian to walk, not after the flesh, but after the Spirit.

Learn these three great lessons: 1. Christians cannot in their own strength love God and all people. 2. The great reason of so much bitterness and want of love, is that Christians walk after the flesh. 3. The only sure way to love God and Christ with the whole heart, to love one another fervently, and to have a tender compassionate love for all who do not yet know Christ – is an absolute surrender to the Holy Spirit.

OCTOBER 4

PASSING THE LOVE OF WOMEN

"My brother Jonathan: thy love to me
was wonderful, passing the love of women."
2 Samuel 1:26

God created man in order to show what the power of love is when a man strives for the welfare of others and even gives up his life for them. He created woman to show what tenderness and quiet endurance are when she sacrifices herself for the sake of others. Dear sisters, preserve as a great treasure the precious jewel which God has entrusted to you – to reflect the love of God in all its tenderness and sympathy. This will give her a heavenly influence and power over her husband and children; and in her dealings with her neighbors, she will be a living witness to what the love of God can do.

OCTOBER 5

STEWARDS OF THE LOVE OF GOD

"Moreover it is required in stewards,
that a man be found faithful."
1 Corinthians 4:2

The minister of the Gospel is a steward of God and above all of the deep mystery of His everlasting love and all the blessings that flow from it. So the minister of the Gospel must himself be faithful not only to God, but to his congregation, caring for the needs of the souls entrusted to him and ready to share God's love with others. This divine love is a mystery and can only dwell in a heart set apart for God and satisfied with His love which flows from Him as a stream of living water. O child of God, seek to have a deeper insight into what the office of a servant of God means, as a steward of the wonderful love of God.

OCTOBER 6

FAITH WORKING THROUGH LOVE

*"In Christ Jesus neither circumcision availeth anything,
nor uncircumcision; but faith working through love."*
Galatians 5:6

Faith is the root; Love is the fruit. Faith becomes strong
in the love of God and of Christ. Faith in God and love to
the brethren must always go hand in hand. Faith in God's
wonderful love, shed abroad in our hearts, enables us to
live always in love towards those around us. This true
faith gives us a power for a life of fervent, all-embracing
love. All of our life should be a life in the love of Christ.
Let our faith each day take deeper root in God's eternal
love. And then each day the fruit of the Spirit will be love
in all our dealings with those around us.

OCTOBER 7

THE DISPENSATION OF THE SPIRIT

*"How much more shall your Heavenly
Father give the Holy Spirit to them that ask Him."*
Luke 11:13

The main thing for us is to receive, afresh from the
Father, the Holy Spirit for our daily needs and daily life.
Without this we cannot please God, nor can we be of any
real help to those around us. Our prayers, if they are to
raise our loves to fulfill God's purpose, must have their
origin in God Himself, the highest source of power. And
so it happens that if the Holy Spirit prays through us, as
human channels, our prayers will rise again to God who
is their source, and the prayers will be answered by the
Divine working in ourselves and in others.

OCTOBER 8

THE FRUIT OF THE SPIRIT

"The fruit of the Spirit is love, joy, peace, long-suffering, gentleness, goodness, faith, meekness, temperance."
Galatians 5:22-23

Think of the first three fruits, *Love, Joy, Peace,* the three chief characteristics of a strong faith life. *Love* to God and to Christ, to other Christians and to all people. *Joy,* the proof of the perfect fulfillment of every need, of courage and faith for all the work we have to do. *Peace,* the blessed state of undisturbed rest and security in which the peace of God that passes all understanding can keep our hearts and minds. Shall we not lay before the Spirit as the great desire of our hearts that He may make these fruits reach perfection within us?

OCTOBER 9

LED BY THE SPIRIT

"As many as are led by the Spirit
of God, they are the sons of God."
Romans 8:14

Let us now consider four other fruits of the Spirit: *Long-suffering, Gentleness, Goodness, Meekness,* all denoting attributes of the Godhead. They will reach maturity in us through much prayer for the working of the Holy Spirit. The Holy Spirit, the gentle dove, longs to impart the ripe fruits of these four attributes of God in our hearts.

Is it not a wonderful thought that these four attributes of God, which are the characteristics of God's work among sinners, may be brought to ripeness in our hearts by the Holy Spirit, so that we in all our ways and conversation may be like the Meek and Lowly One.

OCTOBER 10

THE SPIRIT OF FAITH

"Having the same spirit of faith, we also believe."
2 Corinthians 4:13

Let us pause a while on the two last fruits of the Spirit –
Faith and Temperance. Faith is a fruit of the Spirit – and
leads the seeking soul to depend on God alone. Faith
believes God's Word and clings to Him and waits in
perfect trust that His Power will work within us all that
He has promised. *Temperance* refers in the first place to
eating and drinking and leads us to restraint, carefulness,
and unselfishness in our conversation, our desires, in all
our dealings with one another. Righteous in the doing
of God's will. Devout in our close communion with God
Himself.

OCTOBER 11

WORSHIP GOD IN SPIRIT

"We worship God in the Spirit, and rejoice in Christ Jesus, and have no confidence in the flesh."
Philippians 3:3

First we come to God the Father thanking Him for all the blessings of this life. We acknowledge our entire dependence and express our trust in His love for us. We wait before Him until we have the assurance that He hears us. Then we direct our prayer to the Lord Jesus and ask for His grace to abide in Him. Lastly, we pray to the Holy Spirit. We ask Him to strengthen us in the faith, that what we have asked the Father and the Son may be truly wrought in us.

We count on the Lord Jesus through the Holy Spirit to work within us.

OCTOBER 12

INTERCESSION

"Pray one for another."
James 5:16

Intercession strengthens our love and faith in what God can do and is a means of bringing blessing and salvation to others. Let us learn the lesson thoroughly: Prayer should not be for ourselves alone, but chiefly for others. Let us begin by praying for those who are near and dear to us, those with whom we live, that we may be of help to them and not a hindrance. Pray for divine wisdom, for thoughtfulness for others, for kindliness, for self-sacrifice on their behalf. Pray for all your friends; for those who do not yet know the Lord as their Savior; pray for all those involved in mission work. Just think what an inconceivable blessing it is to help souls through your prayers.

OCTOBER 13

TIME

"What, could ye not watch with me one hour?"
Matthew 26:40

Dear child of God, let us never say, "I have no time for God." Let the Holy Spirit teach us that the most important, the most blessed, the most profitable time of the whole day is the time we spend alone with God. Pray to the Lord Jesus who in His earthly life experienced the need of prayer, pray to the Holy Spirit who will impress upon us this divine truth. As indispensable to me as the bread I eat and the air I breathe, is communion with God through His Word and prayer. Whatever else is left undone, God has the first and chief right to my time. Then only will my surrender to God's will be full and unreserved.

OCTOBER 14

THE WORD OF GOD

"The Word of God is living and active."
Hebrews 4:12

Prayer is like fire. The fire can only burn brightly if it is supplied with good fuel. That fuel is God's Word which must not only be studied carefully and prayerfully, but must be taken into the heart and lived out in the life.

Each word of promise of God is a seed containing a divine life in it. If I carry it in my heart by faith, love it and meditate on it, it will slowly but surely spring up and bring forth the fruits of righteousness. Prayer is the expression of our human need and desire. The Word of God is the means that the Holy Spirit teaches us to use as a guide to what God will do for us.

OCTOBER 15

IN THE NAME OF CHRIST

"Whatsoever ye do, in word or in deed, do all in the Name of the Lord Jesus, giving thanks to God the Father through Him."
Colossians 3:17

At first it may seem impossible to remember the Lord Jesus in everything and to do all in His Name, yet the mere endeavor will strengthen us. The love of Christ will enable us to live all day in His Presence. We need to completely surrender ourselves to live for God all the day.

The man who does all in word and deed, in the Name of Jesus, may have the full, childlike confidence that what he asks in that Name, he will receive. Take the text into your heart, and you may count on the Holy Spirit to make it true in your life.

OCTOBER 16

THE SPIRIT GLORIFIES CHRIST

"He shall glorify Me, for He shall take of Mine, and shall declare it unto you."
John 16:14

Where there is an earnest desire for the glory of Jesus in the heart of the believer, the Holy Spirit will preserve the holy Presence of Jesus in our hearts all the day. We must quietly endeavor to abide in fellowship with Christ always, to love Him and keep His commandments, and to do anything, in word or deed, in the Name of Jesus. If our thoughts are always occupied with the Lord Jesus, His love, His joy, His peace – then the Holy Spirit will graciously bring these fruits to ripen within us. The great desire of the Holy Spirit and of the Father is that Christ may be glorified in and through us.

OCTOBER 17

PRAYING IN THE SPIRIT

"Praying in the Spirit, keep yourselves in the love of God."
Jude 20-21

The Spirit comes to be our life-companion. He wants us wholly in His possession at all times, otherwise He cannot do His work in us. Many Christians do not grasp the truth that He must dwell in them continually and have full possession of all their being. When once this truth is grasped, we shall realize that it is possible to live always "praying in the Spirit." By faith we may have the assurance that the Spirit will keep us in a prayerful attitude and make us realize God's presence, so that our prayer will be the continual exercise of fellowship with God and His great love.

OCTOBER 18

THE TEMPLE OF GOD

"Know ye not, that ye are the temple of God, and
that the Spirit of God dwelleth in you?"
1 Corinthians 3:16-17

From eternity it was God's desire to create man for a dwelling in which to show forth His glory. This is what is prayed for so earnestly: that Christ might dwell in our hearts through faith. This is what our Lord Himself promised.

It is through the Holy Spirit that you will be sanctified into a temple of God, and you will experience that Christ, with the Father, will take up His abode in your heart. Do you desire that the Holy Spirit should teach you to pray? He will do it on this one condition, that you surrender yourself wholly to His guidance.

OCTOBER 19

THE FELLOWSHIP OF THE SPIRIT

"The Communion of the Holy Spirit be with you."
2 Corinthians 13:14

In this verse we have one of the chief characteristics and activities of the Holy Spirit. It is the Holy Spirit through whom the Father and Son are one and through whom they have fellowship with each other in the Godhead. For the Holy Spirit is the true life of the Godhead. Through the Spirit we know and experience the fellowship of love in the life with the Father and Son. Through the Spirit, we, as God's children, have fellowship one with another. In the child of God there should be nothing of the selfishness and self-interest that seeks its own welfare. We are members of one Body. And through the Spirit the unity of the Body must be maintained.

OCTOBER 20

WITH THE WHOLE HEART

*"Ye shall seek Me, and find Me, when ye
shall search for Me with all your heart."*
Jeremiah. 29:13

If one seeks to perform any great work, he must do it
with his whole heart and with all his powers. In worldly
affairs this is the secret of success and victory. In divine
things, it is indispensable, especially in praying for the Holy
Spirit. Have you ever realized when you pray for the Holy
Spirit, *that you are praying for the whole Godhead to take
possession of you?* What God commands and demands
of us, *He will Himself work within us.* On our part there
must be earnest prayer each day and an acceptance of
the Holy Spirit as our Leader and Guide.

OCTOBER 21

THE LOVE OF
GOD IN OUR HEARTS

*"The love of God hath been shed abroad in our hearts
through the Holy Spirit, which is given unto us."*

Romans 5:5

We need time for retirement from the world and its
interests for our souls to bask in the light of God so that
the eternal love may take possession of our hearts. If we
believe in the infinite love of God and the divine power
with which He takes possession of the heart, then we will
receive what we ask for – the love of God shed abroad
in our hearts by the Holy Spirit.

Draw nigh to God and abide with Him in quiet worship and adoration, and you will know the love of God
in Christ.

October 22

Walk in the Spirit

"If we live in the Spirit, let us also walk in the Spirit."
Galatians 5:25

God gives us His Spirit to be in us the whole day. We need Him most in the midst of our daily work because the world has then such power to lead us away from God. We need to pray to the Father every morning for a fresh portion of His Spirit for each day. As long as we are not under the guidance of the Holy Spirit, the flesh will rule over us. Oh, that we knew the unspeakable grace that God has given us! The Spirit in our hearts will cry "Abba, Father," so that we may walk the whole day in God's presence as His beloved children. The Spirit is given you that you may walk by the Spirit at all times.

OCTOBER 23

THE SPIRIT PROMISED
TO THE OBEDIENT

*"If ye love Me, ye will keep My commandments. And I will
pray the Father, and He shall give you another Comforter."*
John 14:15 16

The Holy Spirit is given us to enable us to do the will
of the Father. The condition is reasonable and just, that
as far as we have kept the commandments through the
Spirit, the Spirit will be granted to us in fuller measure.
Let us say to God that we accept the condition with all
our heart and will strive to keep His commands and
ask for power to do His commandments more perfectly.
Surrender yourself unreservedly to the Lord.

OCTOBER 24

SPIRITUAL OR CARNAL?

*"And I, brethren, could not speak unto you as unto spiritual,
but as unto carnal, even as unto babes in Christ."*
1 Corinthians 3:1

God calls us and the Spirit draws us to be spiritual men
and women – people who pray each day to be led and
guided each day into a truly spiritual life. The Spirit will be
granted anew each day if we yield ourselves unreservedly
to be sanctified in all our walk and conversation.

When you pray, entrust yourself fully to the guidance of
the Holy Spirit for the whole day. If there is true willingness
on your part, then the Holy Spirit will take full possession
of you and will preserve and sanctify your life.

OCTOBER 25

THE SPIRIT OF WISDOM

"That the Father may give unto you a spirit of
wisdom and revelation in the knowledge of Him."
Ephesians 1:17-18

Only through the Holy Spirit can the Christian appropriate
the divine truth contained in God's Word. Paul teaches
us that when we read God's Word or meditate on it, we
should pray "Father, grant me the spirit of wisdom and
revelation." As we do this we shall find that God's Word
is living and powerful and will work in our hearts. God's
commands will be changed into promises. The Holy Spirit
will teach us to do lovingly and joyfully all that He has
commanded.

OCTOBER 26

THE SPIRIT OF SANCTIFICATION

"Elect, through sanctification of the Spirit, unto
obedience and sprinkling of the blood of Christ."
1 Peter 1:2

The great work of the Holy Spirit is to glorify Christ in us as our Sanctification. When you once understand that He has the name of Holy Spirit in order definitely to impart God's holiness and will sanctify you wholly, then you will begin to realize that the *Holy* Spirit dwells in your heart. And what will be the result? You will feel that He must have you wholly. My whole life and conversation must be in the Spirit. My prayer, my faith, my fellowship with the Father, and all my work in God's service must be completely under His sway. As the Spirit of holiness, He is the Spirit of my sanctification.

OCTOBER 27

RIVERS OF LIVING WATER

"He that believeth on Me, out of
him shall flow rivers of living water."
John 7:38

What do we need in order to experience these two wonderful promises of the well of water and the rivers of living water? Just one thing – *the inner attachment to Christ and the unreserved surrender to fellowship with Him and the firm assurance that His Spirit will work in us what we cannot do.* In one word: He that believeth on Me. We need a faith that rejoices in the divine might and love and depends on Him day by day to grant us grace that living water may flow forth from us. The union between you and Christ must be uninterrupted; your faith must accept Christ and depend on Him.

OCTOBER 28

JOY IN GOD

*"For the kingdom of God is righteousness
and peace and joy in the Holy Spirit."*
Romans 14:17

Many Christians do not understand that the joy of the Lord will keep them and fit them for their work. To many the thought of the Holy Spirit is a matter of grief and self-reproach, of desire and disappointment, of something too high and holy for them. The kingdom of God is pure joy and peace through the Holy Spirit, and God will fill us with "all joy and peace in believing," (Rom. 15:13) *"through the power of the Holy Spirit."* Pray in all humility to the Holy Spirit, believing firmly that He will lead you into the joy of the Lord.

OCTOBER 29

ALL THE DAY – EVERY DAY

"Every day will I bless Thee."
Psalm 145:2

It is a step forward in the Christian life when one definitely decides to seek to have fellowship with God in His Word each day without fail. A man who had undergone a serious operation asked his doctor, "How long will I have to lie here?" And the answer came: "Only a day at a time." And that is the law of the Christian life. God gave the manna daily, the morning and evening sacrifice on the altar – by these God showed that His children should live by the day. Seek this day to trust to the leading of the Holy Spirit the whole day. You need not care for the morrow, but rest in the assurance that He who has led you today will draw still nearer tomorrow.

OCTOBER 30

THE SPIRIT AND THE CROSS

*"The blood of Christ, who through the Eternal
Spirit offered Himself without blemish
unto God, shall cleanse your conscience."*
Hebrews 9:14

How is it so few Christians understand or experience that
the fellowship of the Spirit is a fellowship of the cross?
Simply because they do not feel the need of praying for
the Spirit of wisdom to give them a deep, spiritual insight
into the oneness of the Spirit and the Cross. Begin today
to ask God to grant you a sight of how the Spirit will take
you to the cross of Christ in fellowship with Him, to die
to the world and to sin, so that all things may become
new, and you will actually live and walk and work and
pray in the Spirit, to the glory of God.

OCTOBER 31

THE SPIRIT AND THE BLOOD

"There are three who bear witness, the Spirit, and the water, and the blood: and these three agree in one."
1 John 5:8

The water is external, a sign of the renewing and purifying through regeneration used in baptism. The Spirit and the blood are two working together in regeneration: the blood for the forgiveness of sins, the Spirit for the renewal of the whole nature. Only through the blood can we with confidence pray for and receive the Spirit. There may be some sin in your life of which you are hardly conscious but which grieves the Spirit. Come with every sin, known and unknown, and plead the blood of Christ as your only claim on the love that accepts and forgives. Accept the fullness of the Spirit to which the blood gives you access.

NOVEMBER

November 1

The Spirit in Preacher and Hearer

"Our Gospel came unto you ... in power, and in the Holy Spirit."
1 Thessalonians 1:5

We are so accustomed to listen attentively to the sermon that we are apt to forget the prayer for the preacher that he may speak "in the demonstration of the Spirit," and then the prayer for ourselves, that we may receive the Word as it is in truth. How earnestly we should pray that God may reveal to us all *"the Spirit of wisdom and revelation,"* that we may discover what the place really is that the Holy Spirit should have in our lives, and what the perfect work is that He will do within us! God help us to learn this prayer!

NOVEMBER 2

THE FULL GOSPEL

"Then Peter said: Repent, ... for the remission of sins,
and ye shall receive the gift of the Holy Spirit."
Acts 2:38

How often only half the Gospel is preached – conversion
and forgiveness of sins, and souls are led no further into
the truth – the knowledge and appropriation of the life
of the Spirit within us is not mentioned. No wonder that
so many Christians fail to understand that they must
depend each day on the Spirit for the joy which will be
their strength. Begin at once to pray the Father to grant
you the gift of the Holy Spirit anew each day. Regard your
heart constantly as a garden of the Lord in which the Holy
Spirit will bear abundant fruit to the glory of God.

November 3

The Ministry of the Spirit

*"Ye are an epistle of Christ, ministered by us,
written with the Spirit of the living God."*
2 Corinthians 3:3

The Corinthian Church was a "letter of recommendation" for Paul. What a wonderful presentation of the work of the minister for his people! A preacher prepared to be a minister of the Spirit, with power to write in the hearts of his people the name and love of Christ. Oh, that all ministers and church-members would unite in the prayer that God would give the ministry of the Spirit its right place and teach the people to believe that when Christ is preached to them, they are beholding as in a glass the glory of the Lord and may be changed into the same image by the Spirit of the Lord!

NOVEMBER 4

THE SPIRIT FROM HEAVEN

*"Them that preached the gospel unto you by
the Holy Spirit sent down from heaven."*
1 Peter 1:12

Christ has taught us to think of God as our own Father who is ready to bestow His blessings on His children. O Christian, take time each day to receive from the Father the continual guidance of the Holy Spirit. Let Him overcome the world for you and strengthen you as a child of heaven to walk daily with your God and with the Lord Jesus. The Holy Spirit will do His part, if you in faith surrender yourself to His control. You will learn to speak to others with such heavenly joy that you will draw them, too, to give themselves to the leading of the Spirit and to walk in the heavenly joy of Christ's love.

NOVEMBER 5

THE SPIRIT AND PRAYER

"Verily, verily, I say unto you, If ye shall ask anything
of the Father, in My Name, He will give it you."
John 16:23

In our Lord's farewell discourse (Jn. 13:17) He presented the life in the dispensation of the Spirit in all its power and attractiveness. One of the most glorious results of the day when the Holy Spirit should come would be: *the new power that man should have* to pray down from heaven the power of God to bless the world. In the power of the perfect salvation that Christ accomplished, in the power of His glory with the Father, in the power of the outpouring of the Holy Spirit to dwell in the hearts of His servants, they would have the unspeakable freedom to ask what they desired and it should be done.

NOVEMBER 6

WITH ONE ACCORD IN PRAYER

"These all with one accord continued steadfastly in prayer."
Acts 1:14

The call comes to each believer to *pray daily with one accord* for the great gift of the Holy Spirit. The power of the first disciples lay in the fact that they *as One Body* were prepared to forget themselves and to pray for the Holy Spirit over all mankind.

O Christian, *daily prayer in fellowship with God's children is indispensable,* and it is a sacred duty if the Spirit is again to come in power. Let not your knowledge of the working of God's Holy Spirit be limited to yourself alone nor even to your Church, but in a world-embracing love of Christ for all God's children and His kingdom over the whole world, pray for power.

NOVEMBER 7

GOD'S PLAN OF SALVATION

"When Christ, who is our life, shall be manifested,
then shall ye also with Him be manifested in glory."
Colossians 3:4

The full Gospel is contained in these words: "Christ is
our life." Many Christians forget this. They believe Christ
died on the cross for them and lives in Heaven for them,
but hardly that Christ is in them. The powerlessness of
the Church is mainly due to this. *We do not realize that
the Almighty Christ dwells in us.* We must know and
experience and testify to this great truth if there is to be a
real and lasting revival in the Church of Christ. Then we
shall know what it is to give ourselves wholly to Christ,
always to abide in fellowship with Him, that His work
may be accomplished through us.

November 8

The Two-fold Life

*"I came that they may have
life, and may have it abundantly."*
John 10:10

Paul speaks of the Christian life of the Corinthians as not spiritual but carnal, as of young children in Christ incapable of assimilating strong meat or understanding the deeper truths of the Gospel. There are some who never advance beyond first principles.

Dear Reader, ask yourself if you are living such an abundant life as Jesus came to bestow? Is it manifest in your love to the Savior and in the abundant fruit you bear to the glory of God in soul-winning? Let Jesus be precious to you, and daily communion with Him indispensable. He will teach you by His Holy Spirit to honor Him by an abundant life.

NOVEMBER 9

LIFE ABUNDANT

*"Where sin abounded, grace did abound more exceedingly:
that, as sin reigned in death, even so might grace reign."*
Romans 5:20-21

That sin abounds we know full well. But do we believe
that "grace abounds more exceedingly" and enables us
to reign over sin?

These words of the Holy Spirit are almost beyond
our grasp. Let us continually take them to God that He
Himself through His Holy Spirit may make them to live in
our hearts. By them, we shall attain to a firm and joyous
faith. With such a God, with such abounding grace – much
more abundant than the easily besetting sin – with such a
Lord Jesus to give grace and cause grace to reign – thank
God, I may believe that life abundant is for me!

NOVEMBER 10

"CHRIST LIVETH IN ME"

"I have been crucified with Christ; yet I live:
and yet no longer I, but Christ liveth in me."
Galatians 2:20

In these words Paul expresses three great thoughts: His third thought, "Christ liveth in me," is the true secret of a Christlike life. Christ was not only crucified for me. He does not live only in heaven to intercede for me. No! Christ *liveth in me.* He Himself said that even as His Father dwelt and worked in Him, even so He dwells and works in us. He is truly the life in us by which we live.

Do not imagine that Christ's life can be manifested in us unless we die to the world and to self. You are crucified with Christ and must experience the crucified life. The rest will follow.

NOVEMBER 11

THE LIFE OF FAITH

*"That life which I now live in the flesh I live in
faith, the faith which is in the Son of God."*
Galatians 2:20

Here we see the great work that faith has to accomplish
in us and for us, in order to allow the living Lord to work
His will in us. Christ will accomplish the work in our
hearts. The only attitude that becomes us is one of trust,
strengthening our faith in the assurance that "He loved
me and gave Himself for me." The child of God needs
time for meditation and adoration, so that the Spirit of
God may reveal to Him how completely He will fill our
being, accomplishing the work in us. Oh, the depth of
the riches of the wisdom and the knowledge of God! Oh,
the depth of the love of God in Christ!

NOVEMBER 12

THE EVER-ABIDING SPIRIT

"The Father shall give you another Comforter,
that He may be with you forever ... He
abideth with you, and shall be in you."
John 14:16-17

Christ abiding in us and our abiding in Him is altogether dependent upon the indwelling of the Holy Spirit. This can only be done each day as we appear in God's Presence by renewing and confessing our faith in the ever-abiding, indwelling of the Spirit. It is through Him we have Christ in our hearts, animating and enlightening us and filling our lives. This can be ours if we come into touch with God in Christ each day, thus receiving fresh power to influence and bless others.

Take time to worship God. Take time to yield yourself to the Holy Spirit.

NOVEMBER 13

CHRIST AND THE SPIRIT

*"He that believeth on Me, out of his belly shall flow
rivers of living water. This spake He of the Spirit"*
John 7:38-39

We must not expect the Holy Spirit always to give us tokens
of His Presence. He will ever seek to fix our attention
upon Christ. The surest way to be filled with the Spirit is
whole-heartedly to occupy ourselves by faith with Christ.
Begin every morning in God's presence, and there commit
yourself to Christ to accomplish His work in you. Believe
firmly that the Triune God works in your heart.

The stronger your faith in Christ the more freely will
the Spirit flow from you. The more you believe in the
ever-abiding Spirit, the more surely you will know that
Christ dwells and works within.

November 14

The Spirit and Christ

"He shall glorify Me; for He shall take
of Mine, and shall declare it unto you."
John 16:14

The fullness of the Godhead dwelt in Christ so that Christ as the life of God might dwell in us. All the life and love of God which the Spirit imparts to us is in Christ. Our whole life consists in Union with Christ. Our first requirement each day is to know that Christ lives in us and that the Holy Spirit will make this an abiding reality.

Count on the quiet unseen working of the Holy Spirit in your heart. Fix your heart upon Christ on the Cross, upon Christ on the throne, in childlike trust that while you do so Christ will be revealed in your heart by the Holy Spirit.

NOVEMBER 15

THE STRUGGLE OF THE FLESH

*"And I, brethren, could not speak unto you as unto Spiritual,
but as unto carnal, as unto babes in Christ."*
1 Corinthians 3:1

The Christian at his new birth receives the Holy Spirit,
and immediately there begins a struggle between flesh
and spirit. So long as the Christian allows the Spirit to
conquer and is led by the Spirit, the power of the Spirit
over him increases, and he becomes a spiritual man.

The flesh is still there and in the flesh is no good
thing, but he learns that it means that his flesh is crucified
as something that deserves accursed death. When the
Christian is ignorant about the Spirit, or disobedient, then
the flesh obtains the mastery and the Christian remains
weak; there is no spiritual growth.

NOVEMBER 16

GO ON TO PERFECTION

*"Let us cease to speak of the first principles
of Christ, and press on unto perfection."*
Hebrews 6:1

Oh, Christian, if hitherto you have been content to know
that you have repented and believe in God and so are sure
of salvation, I beseech you, do remember this is only the
beginning of eternal life. Listen to the call to press on to
perfection. This is what God desires and what the Son
Himself will do for you. Learn to yield yourself fully to
Christ and to find daily in Him the hidden life, so that
you may grow in grace and God may use you as a soul-
winner. Nothing less than this conformity to Jesus Christ
should satisfy you – a life wholly dedicated to God and
to His dear Son.

351

NOVEMBER 17

THE BUILDING AND
ITS FOUNDATION

"Let us press on to perfection, not laying again the founda-tion of repentance from dead works, and of faith toward God."
Hebrews 6:1

Justification and peace with God are only the beginning. It is union with the crucified and risen Christ that sets us free from the power of sin. This life in Christ is the edifice that must be built upon the foundation of Justification. We must experience that Christ is our life, that we are crucified with Him and in Him are dead and risen again. That only will enable us to live a holy, godly life in the joy of the Holy Spirit.

NOVEMBER 18

THE REFORMATION

"For other foundation can no man lay, than that which is laid, which is Jesus Christ; but let each man take heed how he buildeth thereon."
1 Corinthians 3:10-11

The great work of Luther and Calvin was to lay anew the foundation of Jesus Christ. We can never thank God enough for the Reformation when Jesus was proclaimed anew our righteousness – our peace with God. That great work of the Reformation took fifty years, yet Calvin himself still felt the need of the people to be taught and trained in the paths of righteousness. So long as the foundation had to be relaid in the full truth of conversion and faith, there was a delay in the building itself on the true foundation – a life of sanctification.

NOVEMBER 19

THE WALK IN CHRIST

*"As therefore ye received Christ Jesus the Lord,
so walk in Him, and stablished in your faith."*

Colossians 2:6-7

Here again we have the two kinds of life. The first includes conversion, forgiveness of sin through the blood of Jesus and acceptance as a child of God. Then comes the second, the walk in Christ. Each day the Christian, by his walk and conversation, proves that he abides and lives in Christ.

Let us thank God for the Reformation as a time when the foundation truth of a crucified Savior was laid, but at the same time let us go on to perfection, to a daily uninterrupted walk in Christ wherein we may abound in faith, experiencing the abundance of grace from the fullness there is in Christ for us to enjoy daily.

NOVEMBER 20

"THE MEDIATOR OF A NEW COVENANT"

"Ye are come to Jesus the Mediator of a new covenant."
Hebrews 12:24

The Mediator is responsible that both sides shall faithfully fulfill the obligations as set forth in the Covenant. Jesus is our surety that God will fulfill His promise. It was in the fulfillment of this promise that He spoke so definitely to His disciples of the keeping of His commandments being the way by which God's designs would be accomplished. Meditate on this until you have the assurance that Christ expects His disciples for love of Him, through the Holy Spirit, to do all that He asks; and through His abiding in their hearts they will unceasingly keep His commands.

NOVEMBER 21

BETTER PROMISES

*"He is the Mediator of a better Covenant, which
hath been enacted upon better promises."*
Hebrews 8:6

Could there be better or more definite promises than
these, that God Himself would put His fear into the
hearts of His people *so absolutely that they would not
depart from Him, and that He would cause them* to keep
His judgments and do them? This is the New Covenant
of which Jesus is Mediator. Through the Holy Spirit He
dwells in us and will keep us from sin, so that we shall
have the desire and the power to do God's will in all
things. The promises are sure. He sees to it that the better
promises are fulfilled to those who whole-heartedly and
confidently desire and claim them from Him.

NOVEMBER 22

FELLOWSHIP WITH GOD

"Our fellowship is with the Father,
and with His Son Jesus Christ."
1 John 1:3

Fellowship with God is the unique blessing of the Gospel.
If preachers are content to speak only of conversion,
forgiveness of sin, and safety after death, they will fail
grievously in their work. Christians must be educated to
practice the Presence of God, to have fellowship with God,
thereby ensuring holy living. Our walk with God may be
as natural and as joyful as a walk in the sunshine.

Fellowship with God is the preacher's only source
of power. A life of close fellowship with the Father and
with the Son lived by the preacher, gives him the right
to win others to the same joyous fellowship.

NOVEMBER 23

THE FULLNESS OF CHRIST

"And the Word became flesh and dwelt among us ...
full of grace and truth. For of His fullness
we all received, and grace for grace."
John 1:14, 16

Read these words again and again until you come under the impression of the supreme fullness of Christ.

I may receive a purse containing very little or nothing at all, or many golden pounds. There is a great difference between the two! And so with us as Christians. Some receive Christ with the forgiveness of sin and the hope of heaven and know little of the fullness of Christ and all the treasure there is in Him. Other Christians are not satisfied until they can say, "Of His fullness have we received."

November 24

The Heavenly Life

"Ye died, and your life is hid with Christ in God. Christ is our life."
Colossians 3:3-4

It takes time and quiet thought and prayer in any measure to grasp this great marvel, that the life Christ lives in the Father is the same life He lives in me. One divine life in the Father and in Christ and in me. When we allow God's Holy Spirit daily to keep alive in us that heavenly life in Christ, we shall grasp what it means to say, "I died with Christ, and I die daily to sin and self and the world in order to make room for that glorious heavenly life that Christ actually lives in me." Thus shall I have courage to believe that Christ lives in me and reigns and works that which is well pleasing to His Father.

NOVEMBER 25

A ROYAL PRIESTHOOD

"Ye are an elect race, a royal priesthood."
1 Peter 2:9

One of the chief reasons for the feeble life in the Church is the mistaken idea that man's happiness is the main object of God's grace. A fatal error! God's aim is far holier and far higher. He saves us on purpose that we in turn shall carry out His purpose in saving others. Each believer is appointed to be the means of imparting to others the new life received in Christ. A royal priesthood! The priestly heart is above all things a sympathetic heart in which the love of Christ constrains us to win souls for Him.

A priestly heart! A heart that has access to God in prayer for those who are yet unconverted.

November 26

"Apart from Me – Nothing"

"He that abideth in Me, and I in him, the same beareth much fruit, for apart from Me ye can do nothing."
John 15:5

"Apart from Me, ye can do nothing." What a cause for humiliation! Because the nature we inherit from Adam is so corrupt that in us – that is, in our flesh – dwelleth no good thing. Nay, more, our flesh is at enmity against God. We are under the power of sin to such an extent that we are unable to do anything well-pleasing to God. What cause for thanksgiving! Christ has united us to Himself and so dwells within us. He may work in and through us each day and all day. This is the secret of the spiritual life: the Lord Jesus working in us, enabling us to do His work.

NOVEMBER 27

THE THRICE-HOLY GOD

"The God of peace Himself sanctify you wholly."
1 Thessalonians 5:23

What inexhaustable words! To sanctify you wholly. How is this work to be done? Your entire spirit and soul and even your body is to be preserved without blame at the coming of the Lord.

How does the Thrice-holy God accomplish this great work of sanctifying us wholly? Through His continual indwelling and fellowship and breathing of His holy life into us. As upon a cold day a man may warm himself by standing in the rays of the sun until its warmth penetrates his body, so the soul who takes time for communion with God becomes permeated with the strength of the Triune Holiness.

November 28

"The Spirit of His Son"

"Because ye are sons, God sent forth the Spirit of His Son into our hearts, crying, Abba, Father."
Galatians 4:6

The Spirit that dwells in you, O child of God, is none less than the same Spirit that was in Christ, the Spirit of God's holiness. I may also rely upon Him as the Spirit of God's Son to reveal Christ in my heart and always to keep alive in me Christ's life. All that Christ has said of His abiding in me and I in Him, the Spirit of Christ will work in me. Through the Spirit, Christ's indwelling becomes an actual experience, and as a result, the mind of Christ and His disposition may be formed in me and become manifest. And futhermore the Holy Spirit will fit me for God's service.

November 29

"Ye Are Bought with a Price"

*"Your body is a temple of the Holy Spirit and ye are
not your own; glorify God, therefore, in your body."*
1 Corinthians 6:19-20

What does the Spirit expect of me? Your body is His
temple. You are not your own, you have no right to please
yourself. You have been dearly bought with the blood of
Christ. The Spirit has absolute right to your whole life.
Therefore you must glorify God in your body and your
spirit. Furthermore He expects that I shall keep in close
touch with Him by taking time to renew the bond between
Him and me. My whole life must be yielded to Him, that
He may bring to perfection in me all His glorious fruits.
The Spirit expects that my body shall be a temple of God
from which praise to God shall continually arise.

NOVEMBER 30

REVIVAL

"Turn us again, O LORD God of Hosts. Cause Thy face to shine, and we shall be saved."
Psalm 80:19

Where must the Revival begin? *With God's children*, who may offer themselves to God as instruments to be used by the Holy Spirit, separating themselves from sin, and devoting themselves to the work of saving souls. Christians must realize and prove that the object of their life is God's service and the saving of those for whom Christ shed His blood. Dear child of God, it avails little to desire a deeper or more abundant life unless this is the chief object: to be a witness for Jesus and to win others to His service and to intercede for them as a labor of love.

DECEMBER

DECEMBER 1

A THREE-FOLD CORD

*"All things whatsoever ye pray and ask for, believe that
ye have received them, and ye shall have them."*
Mark 11:24

To know, To feel, To will, these are the three chief activities
of the soul. These three words will show us the way to
participate in the fullness of Christ. *To know* – We must
see to it that we know clearly what God promises to
do in us, and what He requires of us. *To desire* – With
our whole heart that for which we pray and be willing
to pay the price for it. *To will* – Only by firmness will
faith have courage to appropriate what God bestows.
The more you cast yourself upon the love and power
of Christ, the sooner you will enter into the rest of faith
that ceases from works and depends upon God to fulfil
His purposes.

DECEMBER 2

THE VINE AND THE BRANCHES

"He that abideth in Me, and I in him,
the same beareth much fruit."
John 15:5

In this parable we see what the new life is which the Lord promised His disciples for the work of the Holy Spirit. It clearly mirrors the life of faith.

1. The one object of the life of faith is to bear "much fruit" to the glory of God the Father.
2. Intimate, continuous fellowship.
3. Divine indwelling through the Spirit.
4. Complete reliance, deep humility, constant dependence.
5. Indispensable obedience.

DECEMBER 3

GIVE TIME TO GOD

*"To everything there is a season, and
a time to every purpose under the sun."*
Ecclesiastes 3:1

Is not the most important matter, for which we must find time, fellowship with God in which we may experience His love and His power? Give God time, I beseech you. You need time to feed upon the Word of God and to draw from it life for your soul. Through His Word, His thoughts and His grace enter our hearts and lives. Meditate upon the Word, and lay it before God in prayer as the pledge of what He will do for you. The Word gives you matter for prayer and courage and power in prayer. Let the Word of God teach you what God promises, what you need, and in what manner God wishes you to pray.

DECEMBER 4

DEEPER LIFE

*"And others fell upon the rocky places ... and straightway
they sprang up, because they had no deepness of earth."*
Matthew 13:5

The seed sown upon the rocky places where the soil was
superficial sprang up quickly, but it withered as quickly
because there was no deepness of earth. We have here
a striking picture of so much religion which begins well
but which does not endure. The way to remain rooted
in love is in humble prayer before God. Commune with
the Christ who loved you with the same love with which
the Father loved Him, that in so doing you may get an
insight into the greatness of that love to you. Only in the
life that knows the powerful working of the Spirit is such
a life rooted in love possible.

DECEMBER 5

SOUL-WINNING

"He that abideth in Me, and I in him, beareth much fruit, for apart from Me ye can do nothing ... Herein is My Father glorified, that ye bear much fruit."
John 15:5, 8

All that the Lord Jesus has taught us about His abiding in us and we in Him is to make us understand that it is not for our benefit, but for His good pleasure and the honor of the Father. We, as branches of the Heavenly Vine, receive and enjoy such astounding grace that we may win souls for Him. Have you not given too much thought to your own sanctification and joy, not remembering that as Christ sought His blessing and glory from the Father in the sacrifice of Himself for us, so we, too, are called to live solely to bring Christ to others?

DECEMBER 6

INTERCESSION

*"If a man sees his brother sinning, he shall
ask, and God will give him life."*
1 John 5:16

The believer who abides in Christ has the right to pray
for souls and Christ and the Father will answer that
prayer. Remember, that you are a branch of the Heavenly
Vine not only for your own salvation, but that you may
bear much fruit in the conversion of souls. It is as an
intercessor that grace is granted you to pray for others,
believing assuredly that God will answer you. Think of
the change that would come over a community if every
believer in it would take time to pray for those who do
not believe. How God would be glorified in our bearing
much fruit!

DECEMBER 7

CHRIST OUR LIFE

"Ye died, and your life is hid with
Christ in God. ... Christ is our life ."
Colossians 3:3-4

Only God's Spirit can enable the believer to grasp and appropriate the truth that he was actually crucified and died with Christ. The new life he receives in Christ through the Spirit is life out of death. In Christ as the Lamb in the midst of the throne, the power of that life is shown as a crucified life in each one who has received it. The Holy Spirit gives me the assurance that I died with Christ, and the power of His death works in me.

What joy to know that the new life of God's children around me is also hid with Christ in God! How sincerely we should love each other and pray for each other.

DECEMBER 8

THE THRONE OF GRACE

*"Unto Him that sitteth on the Throne, and unto
the Lamb, be the blessing, and the honor, and
the glory, and the dominion, forever and ever."*
Revelation 5:13

The Throne of Grace, the Throne of God and of the Lamb.
The three-fold song is the heavenly chorus which was
sung at the dedication of the Throne of Grace to the
glory of God and of the Lamb. When you draw near to
the Throne of Grace, think of what it cost Christ to found
that Throne, and what assurance it gives that you will
find grace to help in time of need. I pray you take time
to come under deep conviction that the Lamb as it had
been slain is on the Throne and will make you and your
prayers acceptable to the Father.

DECEMBER 9

THE LAMB IN THE
MIDST OF THE THRONE

"Having then a great High Priest, Jesus the Son of God ...
Let us draw near with boldness unto the Throne of Grace."
Hebrews 4:14-16

The holy God has done His utmost to draw us to Himself and grant us heavenly boldness to pray with the assurance that our defective prayers, will find acceptance with God the Father. O, take time in deepest humility and childlike faith and with all the love of which your heart is capable to worship Him as your Surety and Intercessor and great High Priest. Your heart will then become a true temple of God where day by day the song will arise. Then we shall have the joy and faith to expect a speedy answer.

DECEMBER 10

ABUNDANT GRACE

"The grace of our Lord abounded exceedingly
with faith and love which is in Christ Jesus."
1 Timothy 1:14

Scripture uses great words to reveal this grace to us. It speaks of "the riches of grace"; "the glory of grace"; "the abundance of grace." What treasures are contained in these words! Let the Holy Spirit write them in your heart, that you may receive the full impression of the "exceeding riches" and the abundance of the glory of the grace to be received at the Throne of Grace. Let the thought take possession of you that all day long the abundance of grace will be granted to the soul who approaches with boldness and is ready to receive from the sympathizing High Priest that which He has to bestow.

DECEMBER 11

"WITH ALL THY HEART"

"Thou shalt love the Lord thy God with all
thy heart, and with all thy soul, and with
all thy mind, and with all thy strength."
Mark 12:30

Our love, our prayers, our consecration, our trust, our obedience – in all these there must be an unreserved surrender to God's will and service. Is He not worthy that all that is within us shall love and honor Him with all our strength and all our heart. Think what it would mean in your prayer-life if you were strengthened with all might to call upon God each day! Take this commandment into your heart and make it the rule of your life and try to realize that God must have all. It will make a great difference in your life, and you will go from strength to strength until you appear before God in Zion.

DECEMBER 12

THE LAMB AND MISSIONARY WORK

"Thou wast slain, and didst purchase unto God with Thy blood men of every tribe, and tongue, and people, and nation."
Revelation 5:9

The Lamb upon the Throne has brought salvation to all the nations and tribes of the earth, and to the Church of the Lamb has been entrusted the distribution of the salvation by the power of the Holy Spirit. May the Holy Spirit imprint deeply in our hearts the wonder of missionary work! Just as the Lamb of God gave Himself to die that He might send the glad tidings to all, let us so offer ourselves wholly and without reserve to live and to die that souls may be led to join in the Song of the Lamb before the Throne of God.

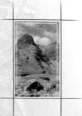

DECEMBER 13

THE LAMB AND HIS WORSHIPERS

"Hast made us unto our God kings and
priests: and we shall reign on the earth."
Revelation 5:10

If we take part with all our hearts in the Song of the Lamb, we shall realize that we are priests of the Throne of Grace. As priests we worship God and the Lamb and with hearts full of adoration may approach the Throne of the Lamb for ourselves and others. As kings we receive the abundance of grace that we may reign in life over sin and the power of the world. The Throne of Grace will become more precious to us as we understand that abundant grace will work within us in greater power when we give our lives to make this salvation known to others.

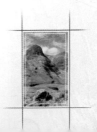

DECEMBER 14

THE LAMB AND THE SPIRIT

"I saw a Lamb standing ... having seven horns,
and seven eyes, which are the seven Spirits of God."
Revelation 5:6

Let us learn two great lessons. The first, that the Lamb on
the Throne has power to fill us with the Holy Spirit and
enable us to follow Him fully and so fit us to commune
with God in the power of the blood and be more than
conquerors. The second, that it is only through the Spirit
that we shall understand the glory of the Lamb and be
filled with His love and so stand firm in the faith of that
which He can do in us and for us and through us.

Do you not long to give Him the place of honor in
your heart and in fervent love submit all that you have
to Him and His service?

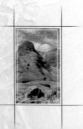

DECEMBER 15

THE LAMB AND PRAYER

"The four-and-twenty elders fell down before the Lamb, having each one a harp, and golden bowls full of incense, which are the prayers of the saints."
Revelation 5:8

All over the world God's children are praying. When with perseverance and faith they entrust their prayers to the Lamb, then in His own time God will graciously send the answer. The Lamb is seated on the Throne with the purpose of drawing out your prayers and strengthening you through His Spirit for more prayer. Let your daily communion with God on the Throne and with the Lamb be a means of receiving from that Throne the rich abundant Grace for your every need.

DECEMBER 16

"THE BLOOD OF THE LAMB"

*"They have washed their robes, and made them white in the
blood of the lamb. Therefore are they before the Throne
of God, and they serve Him day and night in His temple."*
Revelation 7:14-15

What a close relationship to the Lord Jesus it gives me
when I know that He has bought me with His blood. O
Christian, just as you are clothed in suitable garments to
meet royalty, so you must each day put on the white robe
which has been washed in the blood of the Lamb. You
then become one of the royal priesthood who serve God
and intercede for souls. The precious blood of Christ gives
us access with boldness into God's presence. It links us
closely to the Lord Jesus and gives us the needed power
that we may be a blessing to others.

DECEMBER 17

FOLLOWING THE LAMB

*"These are they which follow the
Lamb whithersoever He goeth."*
Revelation 14:4

The Lamb on the Throne has power to lead me and fashion me according to His own image. The Lamb on the throne of my heart is able to increase His own meekness and self-sacrifice within me, and His love to the Father and His redeemed ones. Follow the Lamb! Let this be our watchword and prayer each day! The Lamb in His perfect innocence and purity. The Lamb in His patience and silence. The Lamb who offered Himself to God as a burnt offering and sweet-smelling incense. The Lamb who was slain for us is now, in the fullness of His grace, in the midst of the Throne, our chief Captain and Perfecter of our faith.

DECEMBER 18

THE VICTORY OF THE LAMB

*"They overcame him [the old serpent, the devil], because
of the blood of the Lamb, and because of the word of their
testimony; and they loved not their life even unto death."*
Revelation 12:11

The Lamb is the Lord of lords and King of kings, and
is the victor over every enemy; and those who are with
Him, the called, the chosen and faithful, reign with Him.
Faith in the power of Christ and His blood – this is the
secret over sin and the world.

Dear children of God be faithful followers of the Lamb.
Let your trust in the wonderful life-giving power of the
blood and the remembrance of all that He has done for
you, be joined to the intense feeling that reckons even
life not too precious to be offered up wholly for Him.

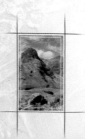

DECEMBER 19

THE MARRIAGE OF THE LAMB

*"Blessed are they which are bidden
to the marriage supper of the Lamb."*
Revelation 19:9

All who rejoice in Salvation are called to the marriage of the Lamb, not merely as spectators, but unitedly they form the bride of the Lamb. What joy there will be when the Everlasting Love shall celebrate its triumph.

O child of God, will you not each day make use of the unspeakable privilege of approaching the Throne of Grace? Will you not pray for grace that each day the way may be made more ready for the great heavenly marriage feast of the Lamb?

DECEMBER 20

THE THRONE OF
GOD AND OF THE LAMB

*"He showed me a river of water of life, bright as crystal,
proceeding out of the Throne of God and of the Lamb."*
Revelation 22:1

What does the river of water of life signify? Nothing less
than the Holy Spirit which was not given until the Lamb
was in the midst of the Throne. Where does the river of
the water of life flow? Through the whole earth. It gives
us according to our faith and desire that which Christ
has promised, a fountain springing up to eternal life. It
is only as we seek with an undivided heart that our eyes
will be opened to see that the waves of the life-stream
flowing from the throne of God and the Lamb are for
our daily use.

DECEMBER 21

THE HEAVENLY LIFE

"They shall see His face; and His name shall be on their foreheads."
Revelation 22:4

Obedience to God's commandments, the abiding in the light of His countenance, has an influence on the character and even the appearance of the children of God. Dear Christian, it is a great thing to approach the Throne of Grace and to receive grace for each day. But there is a still greater blessing when the face of God and of the Lamb are revealed to our earnest gaze, and we walk each day in their light. When the Name of Christ is engraved upon our hearts and upon our foreheads, then we are changed into His image from glory to glory.

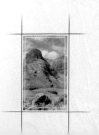

DECEMBER 22

THE REIGN OF GRACE

*"They that receive the abundance of grace
shall reign in life through Jesus Christ."*
Romans 5:17

It is God's will that His children should be conquerors in their life here upon earth. But on one condition – that they should day by day live in the abundance of grace that is to be obtained at the Throne of Grace. Whatever I may know or feel of the power of sin in the world or in myself, I know too that grace is stronger, grace always has the victory over sin. They that receive the abundance of grace reign already in this life through Jesus Christ. Everything depends on appearing daily before the Throne of Grace with a deep sense of need but fully assured that abundant grace will be given us.

DECEMBER 23

PENIEL: FACE TO FACE

"I have seen God face to face, and my life is preserved."
Genesis 32:30

In these words of Jacob we find expression of that which prayer meant to him. The words show us what each child of God, through the grace of God and the power of the Holy Spirit, may experience each day. God will cause His face to shine upon us; we shall see Him face-to-face and be delivered.

Dear children of God, I bring you the message that your Father in heaven is not only willing but greatly desirous that the light of His countenance shall rest upon you. Persevering prayer is needed to bring the soul into the steadfast conviction that God will really make Himself known.

DECEMBER 24

"I AM THE LORD, AND THERE IS NONE ELSE"

*"Jesus answered, The first of all the commandments is:
Hear, O Israel! The Lord our God, the Lord is One."*
Mark 12:29

Love can be called forth only by that which is worthy of love. Love to God can be born only of the knowledge of Him as the one true God in His excellent greatness and glory, His unspeakable love and compassion. Dear reader, here you have the secret of the prayer-life – to meet God each day, to live in the light of His love, to draw near in an absolute surrender to His will. We shall attain to this only as we daily approach the Throne of Grace with boldness. Let this be the great object of your life.

DECEMBER 25

THE ABIDING PRESENCE OF GOD

*"The LORD is nigh unto all them that call
upon Him, to all that call upon Him in truth."*
Psalm 145:18

Prayer has a wonderful power of helping us to draw near
to God and keeping us in His presence. God is everywhere
and as the Almighty One is ever ready and able to grant
us unbroken fellowship with Him. Would you know
the secret of always abiding in a state of prayerfulness?
Realize first that God is near you and within you, then
you will feel how natural it is to talk with Him each
moment about your needs and desires. The principle of
complete dependence on the unseen God and the holy
habit of claiming His presence with us each moment of
the day – this is the secret of a life of true godliness.

DECEMBER 26

TAKE TIME WITH GOD

*"To everything there is a season, and a
time to every purpose under the heaven."*
Ecclesiastes 3:1

It should be the aim of every Christian to set aside a
little time each day for quiet communion with God. We
should live in constant fellowship with Him, but each
day there should be a special time of quiet when we
are with Him alone. Think of the hours per day for so
many years that a child spends at school gathering the
rudiments of knowledge. How much longer then should
we spend in learning from God for life everlasting? O
Christian, give the holy, gracious God all the time you
can until His light and life and love fill your whole life
and you abide in Christ and His love through His Word
and through prayer.

DECEMBER 27

THE WILL

"All Judah rejoiced, for they had sought Him with their whole desire; and He was found of them."
2 Chronicles 15:15

The will is the royal faculty of the soul; it rules over the whole man. Many Christians make no advance in their prayer-life because they have not the courage to say with a strong purpose of will: "By God's help I will do all that God's Word and my own conscience bid me do. I will make time for prayer and quiet fellowship with Him." God is willing to bless you but is unable to do so as long as you are not willing to give yourself unreservedly and with all the strength of your will to let Him work out His will in you.

DECEMBER 28

CHRIST'S LOVE TO US

*"A new commandment I give unto you, That
ye love one another, even as I have loved you."*
John 13:34

God sent His Son to earth to manifest His love. The same
love that God had to His Son, He had in His heart to all
mankind. This same love Jesus exercised toward His
disciples. This love was given to them when the Holy
Spirit was poured out. A living, divine power, flowing
from the Father to the Son and so streaming forth to the
whole world. The Holy Spirit, as the power of this holy
love, sheds it abroad in our hearts. He who meditates
on it until he believes it will have courage to bring his
petitions to the Throne of Grace and to receive the love
which passes all understanding.

December 29

Our Love to Christ

"If ye love Me, ye will keep My commandments."
John 14:15

The Father and the Son dwell in the hearts of those who love Jesus and keep His commandments. Such can say with St. Paul, "Christ lives in me," and I will love the brethren and all around them with the love wherewith God loved His Son. Many Christians do not realize the love Christ has for them. If we are strengthened through the Holy Spirit, Christ will dwell in our hearts, and we shall be rooted and grounded in love. Then it will be quite natural for the love of God to work within us in divine power. Dear Christian, as Christ loved you and you abide in His love, you will be enabled to keep His commandments.

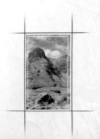

DECEMBER 30

OUR LOVE TO THE BRETHREN

"Love one another, even as I have loved you."
John 15:12

The Lord came to earth to make known God's love to us. He had revealed the love of God the Father and would leave this love on earth in charge of His disciples. He said to them: "As you love others in the power of my love, they will also grow strong to love. And this will be a powerful sign that my love is in you, when the world is convinced the Father has shed abroad His love." Child of God, bow at the feet of your blessed Lord and worship and adore Him for His wonderful grace, and He will take up His abode in your heart in the love of the Father and give you the love wherewith to love your brethren and so prove to the world that God is truly in our midst.

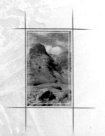

DECEMBER 31

LOVE DEMANDS ALL

"Hereby know we love, because He laid down His life for us; and we ought to lay down our lives for the brethren."
1 John 3:16

The strength of God's love in Christ enabled Him to give up His life wholly for us. The same strength is available for us, and as we yield ourselves wholly to it, we shall be able to make the welfare of souls the central object of our lives. One who gives himself wholly into the keeping of God's love will feel its power and all-sufficiency. This is the blessedness of the Christian life – giving our lives wholly for others even as Christ did. The example of Christ bids us give our whole life in service to our brethren. The love of Christ constrains you and will supply all the power and strength needed.